Michael M. Dediu

Archimedes to Ford:
Invention History
celebrated after 1943

A chronological and photographic documentary

DERC Publishing House
Tewksbury (Boston), Massachusetts, U. S. A.

Published and printed in the
United States of America
On the Great Seal of the United States are included:
E Pluribus Unum (Out of many, one)
Annuit Coeptis (He has approved of the undertakings)
Novus Ordo Seclorum (New order of the ages)

Library of Congress Control Number: 2019904108

Dediu, Michael M.

Archimedes to Ford: Invention History celebrated after 1943
A chronological and photographic documentary

ISBN-13: 978-1-939757-88-3

Preface

From Plato it is well known, for over 2360 years, that the necessity is the mother of invention. Then Archimedes, over 2230 years ago, clearly stated: ***"Give me a lever long enough and a fulcrum on which to place it, and I shall move the world",*** and ***"There are things which seem incredible to most people who have not studied Mathematics".***

Starting with the invention of languages, Archimedes' screw, and Heron engine, there are many wonderful discoveries presented here, which help us to understand how we arrived at the current advanced level of technology. Do you remember Huygens, Hertz, Cartwright, Volta, Babbage and Cerf? They, and many others, will be happy to tell you about their inventions. Is there a connection between The Count of Monte Cristo and Chappe's invention? This book will surprise you.

Starting from 1943, in a chronological order, we present the invention history, which was commemorated in the last 76 years. There are also many attractive and historic photographs – I want to thank my wife for her photo assistance.

This book, for the general public, reminds us of the influential innovators who changed our world, and offers a variety of relevant information not only about them, but also about numerous other personalities and important events.

The more you read, the more you'll love it!

Michael M. Dediu, Ph. D.

Tewksbury (Boston), U. S. A., 15 April 2019

New York in 2007: West 42nd Street near 7th Avenue and Times Square, with many tall buildings around, like the Conde Nast Building (1996-1999, 264 m, 48-story office tower, on the left).

Table of Contents

Tokyo (1150) in 2008: Tokyo Metropolitan Gov. Bldg., 243 m, 48 fl, 1991, in Shinjuku, two observation decks on floor 45, 202 m.

Chapter 1. 1943 – 1952: Archimedes, da Vinci, Torricelli, Lavoisier, Volta, Röntgen, Edison, Ford

1943 – Cartwright, Senefelder, Masuoka, Cerf

- circa 300,000 years ago the languages were invented

- circa 2300 years ago, in circa 357 BC the animal-driven rotary mill was invented in Carthage (now northeastern Tunisia and southern Spain).

- circa 2200 years ago, in circa 257 BC the Archimedes' screw was invented by Archimedes at the age of 30.

- about 900 years ago, around 1043, the movable type was invented by Bi Sheng, 53, (990 – 1051, aged 61) during the Song Dynasty in China. Bi Sheng's system was made of Chinese porcelain.

- 300 years ago, in 1643, Evangelista Torricelli, 35, (15 October 1608 – 25 October 1647, aged 39 years and 10 days), invented the barometer.

- 24 April - 200th anniversary of the birth of Edmund Cartwright (24 April 1743 – 30 October 1823, aged 80.5), English inventor and clergyman, who graduated from Oxford University very early, and invented the power loom in 1789 (age 46). Married to local Elizabeth McMac at 19, he was the younger brother of Major John Cartwright (17 September 1740 – 23 September 1824, aged 84 years and 6 days), a political reformer and radical, and George Cartwright (12 February 1739 – 19 May 1819, aged 80.2) explorer of Labrador.

- 26 August – 200th anniversary of the birth of Antoine-Laurent de Lavoisier (also Antoine Lavoisier; 26 August 1743, Paris, France – 8 May 1794, Paris, France, aged 50.7), French chemist and nobleman, who was central to the 18th-century chemical development, and who had a large influence on both the history of chemistry, and the history of biology. He is considered the "father of modern chemistry". Lavoisier discovered the role oxygen plays in combustion, and recognized and named oxygen (1778), and hydrogen (1783). Lavoisier helped construct the metric system, wrote the first extensive list of elements, and helped to reform chemical nomenclature. He predicted the existence of silicon (1787), and was also the first to establish that sulfur was an element (1777) rather than a compound. He discovered that, although matter may change its form or shape, its mass always remains the same.

- 6 November – 172nd anniversary of the birth of Alois Senefelder (6 November 1771 – 26 February 1834, aged 62.3) German engineer, actor and playwright, who invented the lithography printing technique in 1796, at age 25.

- 8 May - Fujio Masuoka was born (8 May 1943, age now over 75.9), Japanese engineer, with Ph. D. from Tohoku University, who invented flash memory in 1980 (age 37).

- 23 June - Vinton Cerf was born (23 June 1943, age now over 75.8), American Internet pioneer, who is one of "the fathers of the Internet" (1975, age 32).

- 6 November – the author was born.

- Winston Churchill, 69, (30 November 1874 – 24 January 1965, aged 90.1), who, 16 years earlier, in 1927 (age 53), wrote to his wife Clementine, 42, (1 April 1885 – 12 Dec 1977, aged 92.7, had 5 children) that he is becoming a film fan, had film projection equipment installed at Chequers, the country home of British prime ministers.

Roma in 2011: Statue of Julius Caesar (100 BC – 44 BC, reign 49 BC – 44 BC), Templum Saturnus (497 BC, center back), Chiesa Santi Luca e Martina (650, left). On the base of the statue: SPQR, G Iulio Caesari Dict Perpetuo (SPQR - S(enatus) P(opulus)Q(ue) R(omanus) - the Senate and the people of Rome). The Julian calendar opened on 1 January 45 BC, and it is almost identical to the current calendar. The month of July was named in his honor.

1944 – Keller, Fenerty

- circa 200,000 years ago the glue was invented (found in Italy)

- circa 2000 years ago, in 56 BC, glass blowing was invented on the east Mediterranean coast (now the Lebanese coast).

100 years ago, in 1844, Friedrich Gottlob Keller, 28, (27 June 1816, Hainichen, Saxony – 8 September 1895, Krippen, Saxony, aged 79.4, German machinist and inventor), at the same time as Charles Fenerty, 23, (January 1821 – 10 June 1892, aged 71.4, Canadian inventor who invented the wood pulp process for papermaking, which was first adapted into the production of newsprint. Fenerty was also a poet (writing over 32 known poems)), invented the wood pulp process for use in papermaking. He is known for his wood-cut machine (used for extracting the fibers needed for pulping wood). Unlike Charles Fenerty, F.G. Keller took out a patent for his wood-cut invention.

Rome (753 BC), Vatican (1929): Piazza di San Pietro (1656 – 1667, Bernini), the south part of the portico of the Basilica Papale di San Pietro (1506 – 1626,), with a private entrance to the Vatican City. A halberdier (left down) of the Pontificia Cohors Helvetica (Pontifical Swiss Guard, from 1506, 135 men), with a halberd.

1945 – Volta, Röntgen, Johnson, Goddard

- circa 50,000 years ago ground stone tools were invented (found in Australia, Japan, and other places).

- 18 February - 200th anniversary of the birth of Alessandro Volta (18 Feb 1745, Como, Duchy of Milano – 5 March 1827, Como, Lombardia-Venezia, aged 82 years and 15 days), Italian inventor of the battery in 1799, when he was 54, and now, thanks to the work of scientists and engineers, the batteries are intensely used for medical applications, and continue to dramatically improve.

Lithium-ion batteries have become the most common rechargeable batteries for consumer electronics and automotive applications, due to their high energy densities, decent power density, relatively high cell voltages, and low weight-to-volume ratios. The increased demand, and the pressure for improving battery performance, have intensified the need for mathematical modeling. Modeling and simulations allow for the analysis of an almost unlimited number of design parameters and operating conditions, at a relatively small cost. Experimental tests are used to provide the necessary validation of the models.

The deep freeze in the U.S., in the week of 28 January 2019, exposed some of the limitations of electric vehicles. Owners of Tesla, Nissan and Jaguar EVs reported a loss of range of as much as 30%, amid the recording-setting low temperatures associated with the Polar Vortex. The problem is that lithium-ion batteries, in general, are most efficient at about 20° C. Still, there is optimism that the next generation of EV batteries will dramatically improve performance, although "solid state" batteries aren't expected to be mass produced until 2022 at the earliest.

- 27 March - 100th anniversary of the birth of Wilhelm Conrad Röntgen (27 March 1845, Lennep, Prussia (now Remscheid, Germany) – 10 Feb 1923, Munich, Germany, aged 77.9), German mechanical engineer and physicist, who, on 8 November 1895, at age 50.6, produced and detected electromagnetic radiation in a wavelength range known as X-rays or Röntgen rays, which became important in medical diagnosis and therapy, an achievement that earned him the first Nobel Prize in Physics in 1901, at age 56.

- 100 years ago, in 1845, Isaac Charles Johnson, 34, (28 January 1811 – 29 November 1911, aged 100 years 10 months and 1 day, British cement manufacturer, and a pioneer of the Portland cement industry), invented modern Portland cement.

10 August - Robert H. Goddard passed away at the age of 62.8 (5 October 1882, Worcester, Massachusetts, – 10 August 1945). He was an American engineer, professor, physicist, and inventor, who built the world's first liquid-fueled rocket. Goddard successfully launched his model on 16 March 1926 in Auburn Massachusetts. He and his team launched 34 rockets between 1926 and 1941, achieving altitudes as high as 2.6 km and speeds as fast as 885 km/h.

3 Nov 2009, Piazza della Liberta, looking east to Porticato di San Giovanni (1533, left), Via Vittorio Veneto (center right back), il Campanile della Chiesa del Duomo (center right up), the column (1539) with San Marco's lion (the symbol of Venezia, right).

.

1946 – **Musschenbroek, Roebuck, Maus**

- circa 40,000 years ago cave painting appears in Spain and Indonesia.

- 200 years ago, in 1746, Pieter van Musschenbroek, 54, (14 March 1692 – 19 September 1761, aged 69.5), Dutch scientist, professor in Duisburg, Utrecht, and Leiden, in mathematics, philosophy, medicine, and astronomy, invented the first capacitor, called the Leyden jar:

- 200 years ago, in 1746, John Roebuck of Kinneil, 28, (1718 – 17 July 1794, aged 76), English inventor and industrialist, who developed the industrial-scale manufacture of sulphuric acid (lead chamber process).

- 100 years ago, in 1846, Henri-Joseph Maus, 38, (22 October 1808 – 13 July 1893, aged 84.7, Belgian engineer), invented the Tunnel boring machine.

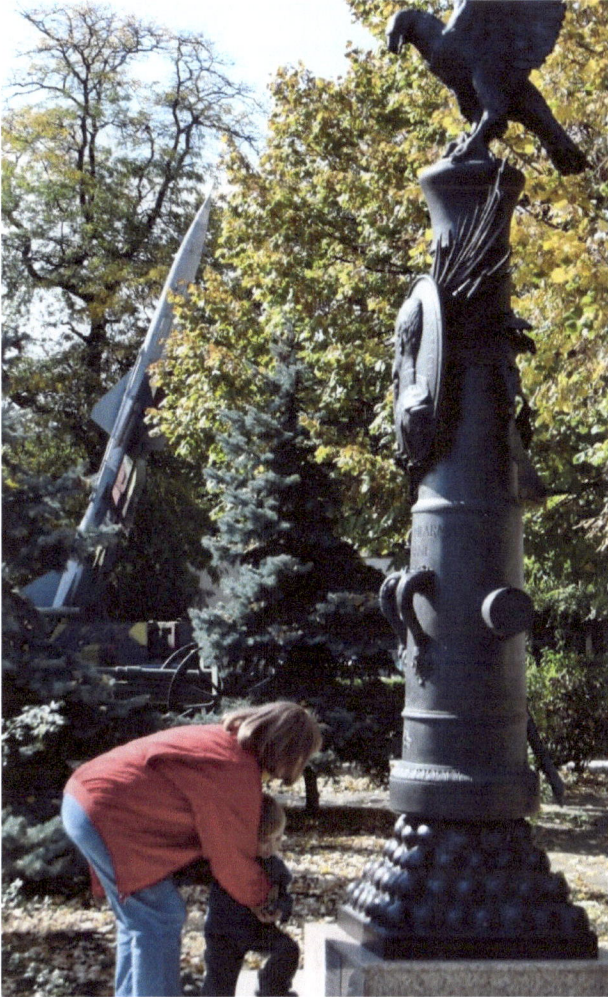

7 Oct 2008, a military monument (right) built with shells at the bottom, an artillery gun barrel, and a vulture on the top, and a two-stage racket (left back). The earliest experiments with multistage rockets in Europe were made in 1551 by Austrian Conrad Haas (1509–1576), the arsenal master of the town of Hermannstadt, Transylvania (now Sibiu/Hermannstadt (1191, elevation 415 m, population 150,000, on Cibin River, 215 km north-west of Bucharest, Romania). There are many contributions to the rocket theory by the Russian Konstantin Tsiolkovsky (1857–1935), the American Robert Goddard (1882–1945), and the German Hermann Oberth (1894–1989), born in Hermannstadt.

1947 – Pacioli, Edison, Ford, Bardeen

- circa 37,000 years ago the mortar and pestle were invented in Southwest Asia.

- 1600 years ago, in 347, oil wells and borehole drilling were invented in China. Such wells could reach depths of up to 240 m.

- 500th anniversary of the birth of Luca Pacioli (Fra Luca Bartolomeo de Pacioli (c. 1447 – 1517, aged 70)), Italian mathematician, Franciscan friar, collaborator with Leonardo da Vinci, and an early contributor to the field now known as accounting. He is referred to as "The Father of Accounting and Bookkeeping", and he was the first author to publish a work on the double-entry system of book-keeping, in 1494, at the age of 47.

- 11 February – 100th anniversary of the birth of Thomas Alva Edison (February 11, 1847 – October 18, 1931, aged 84.6), American inventor and businessman, who is America's greatest inventor. He developed many devices that greatly influenced life around the world, including the phonograph (1877, age 30), the motion picture camera, and the practical electric light bulb.

7 April - Henry Ford passed away at the age of 83.6 (July 30, 1863 – April 7, 1947). He developed the first mass produced automobile, the Model T, which was introduced in 1908, when he was 45, and designed to put average Americans in his cars. Its price regularly dropped over the years it was on the market, as Ford focused on developing transportation that working people could afford.

- December - Invention of the first practical transistor by John Bardeen, 39, (23 May 1908 – 30 January 1991, Boston, Mass, aged 82.7, American physicist and electrical engineer; he is the only person to be awarded the Nobel Prize in Physics twice: first in 1956 (age 48) with William Shockley and Walter Brattain for the invention of the transistor; and again in 1972 (age 64) with Leon N. Cooper and John Robert Schrieffer for a fundamental theory of conventional superconductivity known as the BCS theory), and Walter Brattain, 45, (10 February 1902 – 13 October 1987, aged 85.6, American physicist at Bell Labs who, along with fellow scientists John Bardeen and William Shockley, invented the point-contact transistor; they shared the 1956 Nobel Prize in Physics (age 54) for their invention), under the supervision of William Shockley, 37, (13 February 1910 – 12 August 1989, aged 79.5, American physicist and inventor; he was the manager of a research group at Bell Labs that included John Bardeen and Walter Brattain. The three scientists were jointly awarded the 1956 Nobel Prize in Physics (age 46)).

3 Dec 2009, from Harvard Medical School looking northeast to the Avenue Louis Pasteur (1822-1895, French microbiologist),

<u>1948</u> – Cough, Durrer

- circa 35,000 years ago weaving appeared close to the Black Sea.

- 100 years ago, in 1848, Jonathan J. Couch of Philadelphia invented the first American pneumatic drill.

- The first atomic clock was developed at the United States' National Bureau of Standards.

- Basic oxygen steelmaking was developed by Robert Durrer, 58, (1890 – 1978, aged 88, Swiss engineer).

Switzerland, Geneva, on Quai du Général Guisan (1874-1960), going southeast, Swissotel (center), Jardin Anglais (left), Place des Florentins (right).

1949 – Jenner, Francis

circa 35,000 years ago the flute was invented south of the Baltic Sea.

- 17 May – 200th anniversary of the birth of Edward Jenner (17 May 1749, Berkeley, Gloucestershire, England – 26 Jan 1823, Berkeley, Gloucestershire, England, aged 73.6), English physician, surgeon and scientist, who, in 1796, at age 47, developed the process of vaccination for smallpox, the first vaccines for any disease. The terms "vaccine" and "vaccination" are derived from Variolae vaccinae, the term devised by Jenner to denote cowpox

- 100 years ago, in 1849, the safety pin was invented.

- 100 years ago, in 1849, James B. Francis, 34, (18 May 1815 – 18 September 1892, aged 77.3, British-American civil engineer who in 1833, at 18, emigrate to the United States, and at 19, in 1834, he got a draftsman job in Lowell, Massachusetts, had six children), invented the Francis turbine in Lowell, Massachusetts. With the incorporation of the Francis turbine into almost every hydroelectric dam built since 1900, it is responsible for generating over 18% of all the worlds electricity. Francis also originated scientific methods of testing hydraulic machinery, and was a founding member of the American Society of Civil Engineers and its president in 1880, at age 65.

USA, 5 Feb 2016, driving in winter 30 km northwest of Boston, on Lowell Street (5 km east of Lowell), in Andover (1642, population 34,000, named after Andover (circa 955, county of Hampshire, 100 km southwest of London, 60 km south of Oxford, England, population 64,000)). The highly selective Phillips Academy Andover (1778, the oldest incorporated high school in the USA) is a College preparatory high school (grades 9-12, 1122 students).

<u>1950</u> – Tacticus, Guericke

- circa 16,000 years ago pottery was invented in China.

- circa 2300 years ago, in 350 BC, the Greek hydraulic semaphore system, an optical communication system, was invented by Aeneas Tacticus, who was a younger contemporary of Xenophon (circa 431 BC – 354 BC, aged c. 77, ancient Greek philosopher, historian, soldier, mercenary, and student of Socrates).

- circa 2100 years ago, in 150 BC, the astrolabe was invented in the Hellenistic world.

- circa 1300 years ago, in 650, the windmill was invented in Persia.

- 300 years ago, in 1650, Otto von Guericke, 48, (20 November 1602 – 11 May, 1686, aged 83.5 (Julian calendar); 30 November 1602 – 21 May 1686 (Gregorian calendar)) invented the vacuum pump (the suction pump existed from antiquity).

<u>1951</u> –

- circa 14,500 years ago bread was invented east of the Mediterranean Sea, now Jordan.

- UNIVAC, the first commercial computer, was produced.

- 20 December - first use of nuclear power to produce electricity for households in Arco, Idaho, USA.

USA, Newport (1639), Rhode Island, St. Mary's Parish (1828, 1848-1852). President John F. Kennedy and Jacqueline Lee Bouvier were married here on Sep. 12, 1953.

1952 – da Vinci, Otis

circa 14,000 years ago dentistry appeared south of the Alps Mountains, now northern Italy.

– 15 April – 500th anniversary of the birth of Leonardo da Vinci (full name Leonardo di ser Piero da Vinci, 15 April 1452, Anchiano near Vinci (25 km west of Florence, on a Tuscan hill, in the lower valley of the Arno River), Republic of Florence (ruled by de Medici) – 2 May 1519, Amboise, Kingdom of France, aged 67 years and 17 days), Italian polymath whose areas of interest included invention, painting, sculpting, architecture, science, music, mathematics, engineering, literature, anatomy, geology, astronomy, optics, botany, hydrodynamics, writing, history, and cartography, but he did not publish his findings. He is the father of paleontology, ichnology, and architecture, and is one of the greatest painters of all time. In 1487, Leonardo da Vinci, 35, drew L'Uomo Vitruviano (the Vitruvian Man, now at Accademia in Venice), which is regarded as a cultural icon, being reproduced on the euro coin, textbooks, etc. Vitruvius was an ancient Roman architect, interested in the proportions of the human body. In 1489 Leonardo da Vinci, 37, dissected for anatomical research, and he also painted Lady with an Ermine, the lady being Cecilia Gallerani – finished by 1490. In 1510, Leonardo, 58, collaborated with Professor doctor Marcantonio della Torre, 29, on his work of theoretical anatomy – until 1511, when Marcantonio della Torre died at the very young age of 30. In 1508 Leonardo da Vinci illustrated the concept of contact lenses.

- 100 years ago, in 1852, Elisha Otis, 41, (3 August 1811 – 8 April 1861, 49.3, American industrialist, founder of the Otis Elevator Company (the company was acquired by United Technologies in 1976.), and inventor of a safety device that prevents elevators from falling if the hoisting cable fails), invented the safety brake elevator.

Leonardo da Vinci, 38, 1490, Lady with an Ermine (the lady being Cecilia Gallerani).

Chapter 2. 1953 – 1962: Maxwell, Fleming, Hertz

<u>1953</u> – Coignet, Sawazaki

- circa 12,000 years ago agriculture develops in the Fertile Crescent (Middle East)

- 100 years ago, in 1853, François Coignet, 39, (10 February 1814 – 30 October 1888, aged 74.6, French industrialist), invented structural prefabricated and reinforced concrete. Coignet was the first to use iron-reinforced concrete as a technique for constructing building structures.

- The first video tape recorder, a helical scan recorder, was invented by Norikazu Sawazaki, Japan.

Japan: the north side of Mt Fuji (3,776 m, 15 km south), from the south of Kawaguchiko (830 m elevation, 100 km south-west of Tokyo), near route 139 Fuji Panorama Line

1954 – Fuller, Chapin, Pearson

- circa 12,000 years ago domestication of sheep appears in Southwest Asia, followed shortly by pigs, goats and cattle.

- invention of solar battery by Bell Telephone scientists, Calvin Souther Fuller, 52, (25 May 1902 – 28 October 1994, aged 92.4, physical chemist at AT&T Bell Laboratories, where he worked for 37 years, from 1930 (age 28) to 1967 (age 65); he helped develop synthetic rubber during World War II, he was involved in early experiments of zone melting, he created the method of transistor production yielding diffusion transistors, he produced some of the first solar cells with high efficiency, and he researched polymers and their applications), Daryl Chapin, 48, (21 July 1906 – 19 January 1995, aged 88.5, American physicist) and Gerald Pearson, 49, (31 March 1905 – 25 October 1987, aged 82.6, American physicist whose work on silicon rectifiers at Bell Labs led to the invention of the solar cell; after 1960 (age 55) he was Professor of Electrical Engineering at Stanford University) capturing the Sun's power. First practical means of collecting energy from the Sun, and turning it into electricity.

Washington, D.C. (1790): the Saturn 5 (1967-1973) aft end, at The National Air and Space Museum (1976) of the Smithsonian Institution, between Jefferson Dr SW and Independence Ave SW.

1955 – Cullen, Maxwell, Fleming

- circa 11,000 years ago domestication of rice began in Asia, now China

- circa 2100 years ago, in circa 145 BC the blast furnace was invented in Ancient China.

- 200 years ago, in 1755, William Cullen, 45, (15 April 1710 – 5 February 1790, aged 79.8, Scottish physician, chemist and agriculturalist, important professor at the Edinburgh Medical School (a leading center of medical education at that time), and inventor)) invented the first artificial refrigeration machine.

- 100 years ago, in 1855, James Clerk Maxwell, 24, (13 June 1831 – 5 November 1879, aged 48.4), Scottish scientist in the field of mathematical physics), invented the first practical method for color photography, whether chemical or electronic.

- 11 March - Sir Alexander Fleming, British physician, microbiologist, and pharmacologist, passed away at the age of 73.6 (6 Aug 1881, Darvel, UK – 11 March 1955, London, UK). His best-known discoveries are the enzyme lysozyme in 1923 (age 42), and in 1928 (age 47) penicillin - the world's first antibiotic substance. He received the Nobel Prize in Physiology or Medicine in 1945, at age 64, with Howard Florey and Ernst Boris Chain.

At the Royal Observatory Greenwich (1676), the official Greenwich Mean Time (GMT was replaced by Coordinated Universal Time (UTC) in 1960) on the Shepherd 24-hour gate galvano-magnetic clock (10:21:42), public standards of length for British yard (0.9144 m), two feet (0.6096 m), one foot (0.3048 m), six inches (0.1524 m) , three inches (0.0762 m, down), height above mean sea level 154.7 feet (47.15 m, on the plaque in the center up).

<u>1956</u> – Huygens, Harrison

- circa 11,000 years ago construction of stone monuments started south of the Black Sea, now Turkey.

- 300 years ago, in 1656, Christaan Huygens, 27, (14 April 1629 – 8 July 1695, aged 66.2) invented the pendulum clock, which was a breakthrough in timekeeping, and became the most accurate timekeeper for almost 300 years). It was first conceptualized 19 years before, in 1637, by Galileo Galilei, age 73, but he did not have time to create a working model.

- 100 years ago, in 1856, James Harrison, 40, (17 April 1816 – 3 September 1893, aged 77.4, Scottish-Australian newspaper printer, journalist, politician, and pioneer in the field of mechanical refrigeration), produced the world's first practical ice making machine and refrigerator, using the principle of vapor compression. in Geelong, Australia.

- The hard disk drive was invented by IBM.

USA, July 1980, from the New York Harbor looking northwest to New York City, and the southeast sides of the twin towers (1973-2001, first, with antenna spire (left), 417 m and second (right) 415 m, the square base for each was 63 m on each side, the core of each tower was 27 m by 41 m, with 47 steel columns). They were part of the World Trade Center (complex of 7 buildings in Lower Manhattan, on 16 acres, with 1.2 M m^2 of office space, 95 elevators).

<u>1957</u> – Geissler, Pasteur, Hertz

- in circa 7000 BC large permanent settlements began east of the Mediterranean Sea, now Turkey and neighbors.

- 100 years ago, in 1857, Heinrich Geissler, 43, (26 May 1814, Igelshieb – 24 January 1879, aged 64.6, skilled glassblower and physicist), invented the Geissler tube, made of glass and used as a low pressure gas-discharge tube.

- 100 years ago, in 1857, Louis Pasteur, 35, identified germs as clause of disease.

- 22 February – 100th anniversary of the birth of Heinrich Hertz (22 February 1857 – 1 January 1894, age 36.8, German physicist, who published in 1888, at age 31, a proof of James Clerk Maxwell's (13 June 1831 – 5 November 1879, aged 48.4) electromagnetic theory of light, in experiments that also demonstrated the existence of radio waves. The unit of frequency, cycle per second, was named the "Hertz" in his honor.

- The first artificial satellite, Sputnik 1, was built and launched by the Soviet Union.

- The first Personal Computer controlled by a keyboard, the IBM 610, was invented by IBM.

On Gagarin (First Man in Space) Terrace, on the southwest part of the South Building (1899) of the Royal Observatory Greenwich (1676), looking northeast to the south part of the west side (right), the west part of the south side (left), and to the statue of Yuri Gagarin (1934-1968, Russian cosmonaut, the first man to journey into space, with Vostok spacecraft, which completed an orbit (1h 48') of the Earth on 12 April 1961. Resting place: Kremlin Wall Necropolis).

<u>1958</u> – Kilby, Noyce, Moore

- about 9,000 years ago, in circa 7000 BC, alcohol fermentation was invented, especially mead, in Asia, now China.

- about 2,000 years ago, in circa 42 BC, trip hammer was invented in China.

- independent invention of the integrated circuit by Jack Kilby, 35, (8 November 1923 – 20 June 2005, aged 81.6, American electrical engineer who took part (along with Robert Noyce) in the creation of the first integrated circuit while working at Texas Instruments (TI); he was awarded the Nobel Prize in Physics on 10 December 2000 (age 77.1)), and Robert Noyce, 31, (12 December 1927 – 3 June 1990, of heart attack, aged 62.5, American physicist who co-founded Fairchild Semiconductor in 1957 (age 30) and Intel Corporation in 1968 (age 41, with Gordon Earle Moore, 39, (born 3 January 1929, now over 90.2 years old, American businessman, engineer, and the co-founder and chairman emeritus of Intel Corporation. He is also the author of Moore's law. As of 2018, Moore's net worth is reported to be $9.5 B.); along with Jack Kilby, he created the first integrated circuit or microchip that fueled the personal computer development and gave Silicon Valley its name).

France, Paris, Tour Eiffel (1889, 324 m, 279 m at the 3rd level, looking north-west): Tour Eiffel shadow (center), Pont d'Iéna over La Seine (left down), Avenue de New York (green, on the north side of La Seine), Jardin du Trocadéro (1878, 1937, with the Fountain of Warsaw (center left)), Palais de Chaillot (center up), Port de Suffren (down left), Port de la Bourdonnais (down right), Ave. d'Eylau (up-left, vertical), Av. Albert de Mun (center right).

1959 – Planté

- about 8,500 years ago, in circa 6500 BC, lead smelting started between the Black Sea and the Mediterranean Sea, now Turkey.

- about 2,000 years ago, in circa 41 BC, the Glanum Dam (or the Vallon de Baume dam), was the first arch dam, built by the Romans to supply water to the Roman town of Glanum, the remains of which stand outside the town of Saint-Rémy-de-Provence, Bouches-du-Rhône, in southern France. It was situated south of Glanum, in a gorge that cut into the hills of Les Alpilles in the Roman province of Gallia Narbonensis. The remains of the dam were destroyed during the construction of a modern replacement in 1891, which now facilitates the supply of water to Saint-Rémy-de-Provence in the Bouches-du-Rhône region of France. Now the dam's reservoir is called in French the Lac du Peirou, and is accessible via the Chemin du Barrage. Overall the dam stood 6 m high with a thickness of 3.5 m. The dam collected water that was fed into an aqueduct that in turn supplied the Roman town of Glanum.

- 100 years ago, in 1859, Gaston Planté, 25, (22 April 1834 – 21 May 1889, aged 55.1, French physicist), invented the lead–acid battery, which eventually became the first rechargeable electric battery, marketed for commercial use, and is widely used in automobiles.

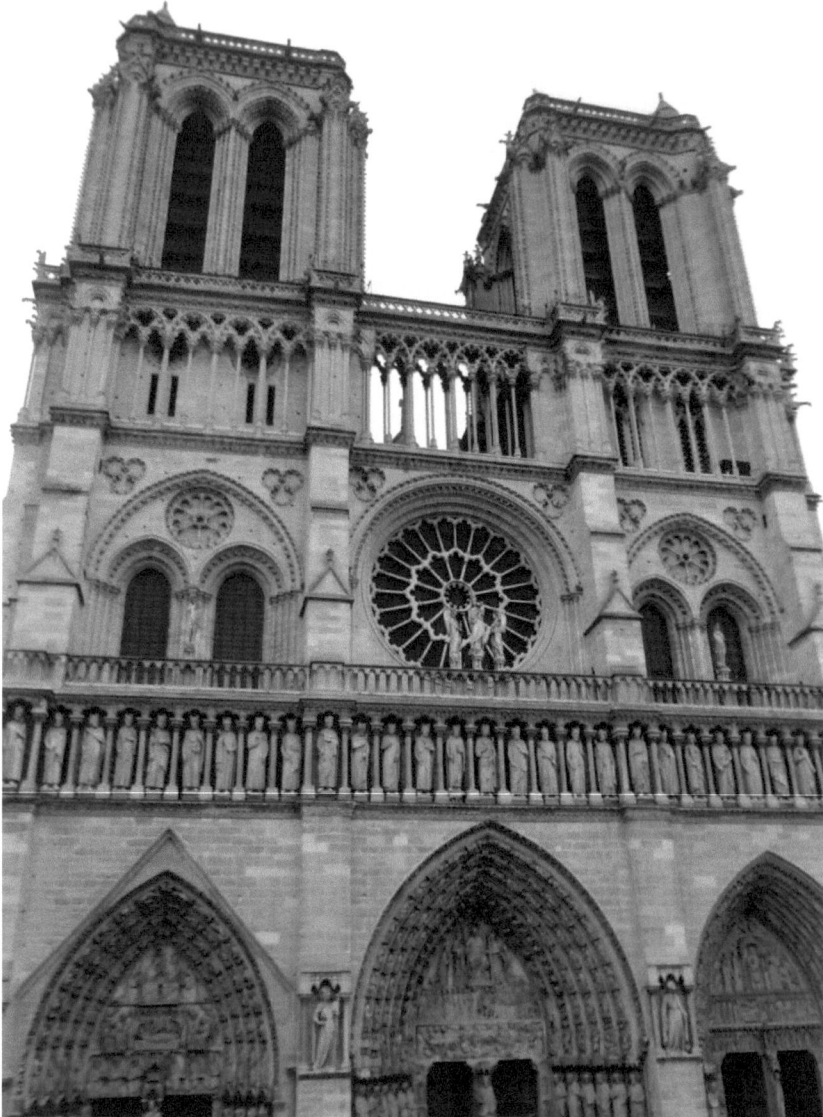

The upper part of the western façade of Cathédrale Notre Dame de Paris (1163 – 1345, 90 m), on the south-eastern part of the Île de la Cité, which is considered the center of Paris, in the fourth arrondissement. The organ has 7,374 pipes, with about 900 classified as historical. It has 110 real stops, five 56-key manuals and a 32-key pedalboard; it is now fully computerized. The Towers at Notre-Dame contain five church bells. The great bourdon bell, Emmanuel, from 1681, 13 t, is located in the South Tower (right).

<u>1960</u> – Swan, Maiman

- in circa 6000 BC kiln was invented in the Tigris – Euphrates rivers area (Mesopotamia), now Iraq.

- circa 2200 years ago, in circa 240 BC the gimbal was invented in Hellenistic kingdoms, and described by Philo of Byzantium (c. 280 BC – 220 BC, aged c. 60, also known as Philo Mechanicus), Greek engineer, mathematician, physicist and writer on mechanics, who lived mostly in Alexandria, Egypt.

- 400 years ago, in 1560, the floating dry dock was invented in Venice, Venetian Republic.

- 100 years ago, in 1860, Joseph Swan, 32, (31 October 1828 – 27 May 1914, aged 85.6, English physicist, chemist, and inventor. He independently developed a successful incandescent light bulb, which were used to illuminate homes and public buildings, including the Savoy Theatre, London, in 1881), produced carbon fibers for the photographic process.

- the first functioning laser (Light Amplification by Stimulated Emission of Radiation) was invented by Theodore Maiman, 33, (11 July 1927 – 5 May 2007, aged 79.8, American engineer and physicist).

UK, London, from a bus on Queen Victoria St, looking west to St Mary Aldemary (a church has been at this site for over 900 years, from around 1100, then rebuilding and restorations took place in 1510, 1629, 1704, 1877, 2005; it is an Anglican church in Bow Lane). In 1781 a new organ was installed, built by George England (1740-1788) and Hugh Russell. The church as rebuilt has an aisled nave, six bays long, with a clerestory.

1961 – Mattessich

- in circa 5000 BC copper smelting was invented in southeast Europe, now Serbia.

- Richard Mattessich, 39, (born 9 August 1922, age now over 96.6, Austrian and Canadian business economist, and Emeritus Professor of Accounting at the University of British Columbia), a professor at the University of California at Berkeley, pioneered the concept of electronic spreadsheets for use in business accounting.

USA, UC Berkeley (1868), from Campanile (1914, 94 m) looking southwest: Bancroft Library (right down), Doe Memorial Library (next up), Herbarium and Museum of Vertebrate Zoology (center), School of Information (left down), English Dep. (next up), College of Letters & Science, German Dep. (center left), Golden Gate Bridge, San Francisco and the Pacific Ocean (up back).

<u>1962</u> – Parkes

- in circa 5000 BC lacquer was invented in southeast Asia, now China.

- 100 years ago, in 1862, Alexander Parkes, 49, (29 December 1813 – 29 June 1890, aged 76.5, metallurgist and inventor from Birmingham, England, had 6 children with his first wife, and 11 children with his second wife, total 17 children), invented parkesine, or celluloid, the first man-made plastic.

UK, London, on the Strand, within the City of Westminster, near the border with the City of London the southwest part of the front of The Royal Courts of Justice (1882, ornate, called Law Courts).

.

Chapter 3. 1963 – 1972: Galilei, Babbage, Pasteur

<u>1963</u> – Guericke

- in circa 4700 BC rowing oars were invented in southeast Asia, now China.

- 300 years ago, in 1663, Otto von Guericke, 61, (20 November 1602 – 11 May, 1686, aged 83.5 (Julian calendar); 30 November 1602 – 21 May 1686 (Gregorian calendar)) demonstrated electrostatic repulsion with his invention of the friction machine.

UK, London, Keats House (1863; at 24 Saint Thomas Street). John Keats (1795 in London – 1821, at 25, in Rome, English Romantic poet) actually lived only six months at 8 Saint Thomas Street.

1964 – Galilei, Pasteur

- in circa 4400 BC the copper sewing needle was invented on the west bank of the Nile in Egypt.

- 15 February - 400th anniversary of the birth of Galileo Galilei (15 February 1564 – 8 January 1642, aged 77.9), Italian polymath. Known for his work as mathematician, astronomer, physicist, engineer, and philosopher, Galileo has been called the "father of observational astronomy", the "father of modern physics", the "father of the scientific method", and the "father of science". He invented the telescope and the microscope, and also created the concept of the pendulum clock in 1637, at age 73, but did not have time to create a working model.

- 100 years ago, in 1864, Louis Pasteur, 42, developed the pasteurization process.

Italy, Naples (Napoli, 1500 BC, one of the oldest continuously inhabited cities in the world. The city was refounded as Neápolis around 550 BC, and became a sine qua non of Magna Graecia), the FVNICOLARE building near downtown. The Funicolare Centrale (Central Funicular) is a funicular railway, which is the main part of the metro system for the city of Naples (1928, 1.2 km).

1965 – Watt, Mendel

- in circa 4000 BC the wheel was invented: first potter's wheels in Mesopotamia (now Iraq), and then wheeled vehicles also in Mesopotamia (Sumerian civilization), the Northern Caucasus (Maykop culture (now Russia)) and Central Europe (Cucuteni (now Romania) – Trypillia (now Ukraine) culture).

- circa 2200 years ago, in circa 235 BC the water wheel and the liquid-driven escapement were invented in Hellenistic kingdoms, and described by Philo of Byzantium (c. 280 BC – 220 BC, aged c. 60, also known as Philo Mechanicus), Greek engineer, mathematician, physicist and writer on mechanics, who lived mostly in Alexandria, Egypt.

- 200 years ago, in 1765, James Watt, 29, (30 January 1736 – 25 August 1819, aged 83.6, Scottish inventor, mechanical engineer, and chemist) improved on Thomas Newcomen's 1712 Newcomen steam engine with his separate condenser. In 1776, Watt steam engines were installed and working in commercial enterprises, which was fundamental to the changes brought by the industrial progress.

- 100 years ago, in 1865, Louis Pasteur, 43, (27 December 1822, Dole, France – 28 September 1895, Marnes-la-Coquette, France, aged 72.7, French biologist, microbiologist and chemist), shows that the air is full of bacteria.

- 100 years ago, in 1865, Gregor Mendel, 43, (20 July 1822 – 6 January 1884, aged 61.5 (Czech composer Leoš Janáček, 29.5, (3 July 1854 – 12 August 1928, aged 74.1, Czech composer, musical theorist, folklorist, publicist and teacher) played the organ at his funeral), scientist, Augustinian friar and abbot of St. Thomas' Abbey in Brno, Margraviate of Moravia. Mendel was born in a German-speaking family in the Silesian part of the Austrian Empire (today's Czech Republic), and gained posthumous recognition as the founder of the modern science of genetics. It was known for long that crossbreeding of animals and plants could favor certain desirable traits, but Mendel's pea plant experiments conducted between 1856 and 1863 established many of the rules of heredity, now called the laws of Mendelian inheritance.), published 'Versuche über Pflanzenhybriden' ("Experiments on Plant Hybridization"), effectively founding the science of genetics, but the importance of his work would be appreciated much later.

UK, London, from Newington Butts, in front of the west entrance to the Elephant and Castle Shopping Centre, a small statue Elephant and Castle, and a tall building (left back) with 3 horizontal holes on top.

1966 – Zernike

- in circa 3500 BC the domestication of the horse began.

- 10 March - Frits Zernike passed away at the age of 77.7 (6 July 1888 – 10 March 1966). He was a Dutch physicist and winner of the Nobel Prize for physics in 1953 (age 65) for his invention of the phase-contrast microscope 36 years ago, in 1930, at the age of 42.

UK, London, from Kennington Road, looking east to the west side of the Imperial War Museum (1917, 1936 in this Bethlem Royal Hospital (1247, 1330, 1815 (this))); on the front (north side, left, Lambeth Road) HEN VIII REGE FVNDATVM CIVIVM LARGITAS PERFECIT

1967 – Priestley, Nobel

- in circa 3200 BC the sailing was invented in ancient Egypt.

- 200 years ago, in 1767, Joseph Priestley, 34, (24 March 1733, England – 6 February 1804, USA, aged 70.9, English, natural philosopher, chemist, and inventor who published over 150 works), invented a method for the production of carbonated water.

- 100 years ago, in 1867, Alfred Nobel, 34, (21 October 1833 – 10 December 1896, aged 63.1, Swedish chemist, engineer, inventor, businessman, and philanthropist; he also owned Bofors, which he had transformed from an iron and steel producer to a major manufacturer of cannon and other armaments. Nobel held 355 different patents, dynamite being the most famous. He bequeathed his fortune to institute the Nobel Prizes, which gave the first Nobel Prizes in 1901), invented dynamite, the first safely manageable explosive stronger than black powder.

USA, the University of California, Berkeley (1868, named after the philosopher and mathematician Bishop George Berkeley (1685-1753), motto Fiat lux (Let there be light), 36,200 students, major public research university, 72 Nobel laureates, between the top six universities in the world, 500 ha campus), il Campanile (Sather Tower (61 bells (full concert carillon) and clock tower). 1914, 94 m, 7 floors, observation deck on the 8th floor, inspired by il Campanile (850, 1514, 1912, 99 m) di San Marco (1084), Venezia (421, Venice), Italy (900 BC)).

1968 – Hahn

- in circa 3000 BC the writing was invented – first cuneiform in Mesopotamia (now Iraq).

- 28 July - Otto Hahn passed away at the age of 89.3 (8 March 1879 – 28 July 1968). He was a German chemist and pioneer in the fields of radioactivity and radiochemistry, considered the father of nuclear chemistry. He was awarded the Nobel Prize in Chemistry in 1944 (age 65) for the discovery and the radiochemical proof of nuclear fission 30 years ago, in December 1938, at the age of 59.

UK, London, at the east end of Westminster Bridge (1862, 250 m, width 26 m, 7 spans, right) over Thames (flowing left to right), Palace of Westminster (1016, 1870, 300 m river front façade, 1,100 rooms, center left, with Victoria Tower (1858, 98 m, left), and Central Tower (91 m)), Big Ben (Elizabeth Tower, 1855, 96 m, center right).

1969 – Mercator, Cugnot

- circa 5,000 years ago, in circa 3000 BC, the tin (stannum) extraction started in Central Asia.

- 400 years ago, in 1569, the Mercator (cylindrical) map projection was created by Gerardus Mercator.

- 200 years ago, in 1769, Nicolas-Joseph Cugnot, 44, (26 February 1725 – 2 October 1804, aged 79.6, French inventor), built the first working steam-powered self-propelled land-based mechanical vehicle, capable of carrying 4 passengers at a speed of 3.6 km/h, the world's first automobile. in 1772, King Louis XV, 62, (15 February 1710 – 10 May 1774, aged 64.2) granted Cugnot, 47, a pension of 600 livres a year for his innovation, known also as "fardier de Cugnot". Following the French Revolution, Cugnot's (64) pension was withdrawn in 1789, and he went into exile in Brussels, where he lived in poverty. Shortly before his death, in 1803, Cugnot's (78) pension was restored by Napoleon Bonaparte, 34, (15 August 1769 – 5 May 1821, aged 51.7), and he eventually returned to Paris, where he died on 2 October 1804.

- ARPANET (Advanced Research Projects Agency Network) first deployed via UCLA, SRI (Stanford Research Institute), UCSB, and The University of Utah. Closed after 21 years, in 1990.

UK, London, from the Shard (2012, 309 m, observatory at 244 m), looking east to the Tower Bridge (1886-1894, combined bascule and suspension turreted bridge over River Thames (flowing from west (left) to east (right)), between London boroughs Tower Hamlets (north – left up) and Southwark (south – right), length 244 m, height 65 m, longest span 82 m, clearance 8 m (closed), 42 m (open)), City Hall (2002, height 45 m, center right round, for the Greater London Authority: Mayor of London and the London Assembly)

1970 –

- Circa 5600 years ago, in 3630 BC, silk garments and sericulture were invented in China.

- circa 5000 years ago, in circa 3000 BC the bronze was invented in Mesopotamia.

- circa 2450 years ago, in circa 480 BC the spiral stairs were invented in Temple A in Selinunte, a Greek city on the south-western coast of Sicily.

- circa 2,000 years ago, in 30 BC, the Ponte San Lorenzo was built by the Romans, being the first segmental arch bridge (3 spans) in the world. It is over the river Medoacus (now Bacchiglione) in Padua (400 km north of Rome, 30 km west of Venice), Roman Republic (now Italy), and was constructed using stones between 47 BC and 30 BC (17 years, there is a bridge inscription). Now the river was filled up to the Riviera del Ponti Romani street. The intact arches of the bridge still exist below street level, and can be visited at fixed times by the public. The Ponte San Lorenzo is 53.30 m long, and 8.35 m wide. The bridge is important in the history of ancient invention and technology for its flattened arches and slender piers. Its three arches span 12.8 m, 14.4 m and 12.5 m, with the span 3.7 times the rise (describing a segment of a circle of 113°). The profile of the structure thus differs from the typical Roman semi-circular bridge arch, with its value of 180°. The pier thickness of the Ponte San Lorenzo measures only 1.72 m, which corresponds to no more than one eighth of the span of the central opening, a value which will not be achieved again for over 1,000 years.

- 1750 years ago, in 220, the woodblock printing was invented during the Han Dynasty in China.

- The pocket calculator was invented in Japan.

Japan, the entrance to a building with a teaching auditorium, 100 m west from the north-east entrance of the Inzai campus of Tokyo Denki University (a private university founded in 1907, and chartered as a university in 1949), 35 km north-east of Tokyo Imperial Palace, 24 km west of Narita International Airport.

1971 – **Farnsworth, Tomlinson**

- circa 5000 years ago, in circa 3000 BC the papyrus was invented in Egypt.

- circa 1300 years ago, in circa 671, the banknote was invented during the Tang Dynasty (618 – 907, for 289 years) in China. Its roots are in merchant receipts of deposit, as merchants and wholesalers desire to avoid the heavy bulk of copper coinage in large commercial transactions.

- 11 March - Philo Farnsworth passed away at the age of 64.6 (19 August 1906 – 11 March 1971). He was an American inventor and television pioneer, who demonstrated the first electronic television to the press 43 years ago, in 1928, at the age of 22. He had 4 sons.

- E-mail was invented by Ray Tomlinson, 30, (23 April 1941 – 5 March 2016, of heart attack, Lincoln, Mass, aged 74.9, pioneering American computer programmer, who implemented the first e-mail program on the ARPANET system, the precursor to the Internet.

- The first commercially available microprocessor, the Intel 4004, was invented.

1972 – Oughtred, Galton, Blanchard, Babbage, Pasteur, Woods, Clark

- circa 5000 years ago, in circa 3000 BC the comb was invented in Persia.

- 1650 years ago, in 322, stirrups were invented in Ancient China: The first dependable representation of a rider with paired stirrups was found in China, in a Jin dynasty tomb, from about 322. The stirrup appeared to be in widespread use across China by 477.

- 350 years ago, in 1622, the mathematician William Oughtred, 48, invented the slide rule: he was the first to use two scales sliding by one another to perform direct multiplication and division.

- 150th anniversary of the birth of Sir Francis Galton, FRS, (16 February 1822 – 17 January 1911, aged 88.9), was an English statistician, polymath, anthropologist, tropical explorer, geographer, inventor, and meteorologist. Galton wrote over 340 papers and books. He also created the statistical concept of correlation and widely promoted regression toward the mean. He was the first to apply statistical methods to the study of human differences and inheritance of intelligence, and introduced the use of questionnaires and surveys for collecting data on human communities, which he needed for genealogical and biographical works and for his anthropometric studies. As an investigator of the human mind, he founded psychometrics (the science of measuring mental faculties) and differential psychology. He devised a method for classifying fingerprints that proved useful in forensic science. As the initiator of scientific meteorology, he devised the first weather map, proposed a theory of anticyclones, and was the first to establish a complete record of short-term climatic phenomena on an European scale. He also invented the Galton Whistle for testing differential hearing ability. He was Charles Darwin's half-cousin.

- 150 years ago, in 1822, Thomas Blanchard, 34, (June 24, 1788 – April 16, 1864, aged 75.8, American inventor who lived much of his life in Springfield, Massachusetts, where in 1819, he pioneered the assembly line style of mass production in America), invented the first pattern-tracing lathe (actually more like a shaper), and was completed for the U.S. Ordnance Dept. The lathe's patent was in force for 42 years, the record for any U.S. patent.

- 150 years ago, in 1822, Charles Babbage, 31, (26 December 1791 – 18 October 1871, aged 79.9, English mathematician, philosopher, inventor and mechanical engineer; had 8 children), originated the concept of a digital programmable computer, is considered the father of the computer, and began building the first programmable mechanical computer.

- 27 December – 150th anniversary of the birth of Louis Pasteur (27 December 1822, Dole, France – 28 September 1895, Marnes-la-Coquette, France, aged 72.7), French biologist, microbiologist and chemist, renowned for his discoveries of the principles of vaccination, microbial fermentation, and pasteurization. He is remembered for his remarkable breakthroughs in the causes and prevention of diseases, and his discoveries have saved many lives ever since.

- 100 years ago, in 1872, J.E.T. Woods and J. Clark (British inventors) invented stainless steel. Harry Brearley (British metallurgist) was the first to commercialize it in 1912.

Italy, Rome (753 BC, one of the oldest continuously occupied cities in Europe, called Roma Aeterna (The Eternal City) and Caput Mundi (Capital of the World)), in Villa Borghese (1630), a monument (1905, by Lucien Pallez, donated by the French Government) to Victor Hugo (1802 – 1885, the greatest French writer (Hernani (1830, inspired opera Ernani (1844) by Giuseppe Verdi (1813-1901)), Notre-Dame de Paris (1831), Le roi s'amuse (1832, inspired opera Rigoletto (1851) by Giuseppe Verdi)), Les Misérables (1862), Les Contemplations, La Légendre des siècles)).

Chapter 4. 1973 – 1982: Pascal, Huygens, Faraday, Maxwell, Bell

1973 – Pascal, Gramme

- circa 5,000 years ago, in circa 3000 BC the star chart was invented in Korea.

- circa 2,000 years ago, in circa 27 BC, the reverse overshot water-wheel was invented by Roman engineers in Rio Tinto, Roman Empire (now Spain).

- 19 June - 350th anniversary of the birth of Blaise Pascal (19 June 1623 – 19 August 1662, aged 39 years and 2 months), important French mathematician, physicist, inventor, and writer. He was a child prodigy, who was educated by his father. He invented the Pascaline or mechanical calculator in 1642, at age 21.

- 100 years ago, in 1873, Zénobe Gramme, 47, (4 April 1826 – 20 January 1901, aged 74.7, Belgian electrical engineer) invented the first commercial electrical generator, the Gramme machine.

- 1 March - the first commercial graphical user interface was introduced on the Xerox Alto.

- The first capacitive touchscreen was developed at CERN (Conseil Européen pour la Recherche Nucléaire - established in 1954, the organization is based in a northwest suburb of Geneva on the Franco–Swiss border and has 23 member states.).

The Institut de France (1795, initially in Louvre, moved in 1805 by Napoléon in this baroque building finished in 1684, for Collège des Quatre-Nations) is a revered French cultural society which includes five académies, the most famous being Académie française (1635) and. Académie des sciences (Academy of Sciences), founded in 1666. The Institute, located on Quai de Conti, manages about 1,000 foundations, as well as museums and châteaux. Its Mazarine Library is France's oldest public library.

<u>1974</u> – Oughtred, Wilkinson, Trouvé

- circa 4500 years ago, in circa 2500 BC the docks were invented in Ancient Egypt.

- around 550 years ago, in 1424, the brace was invented in Flanders, Holy Roman Empire.

- 5 March - 400th anniversary of the birth of William Oughtred (5 March 1574 – 30 June 1660, aged 86.2), English mathematician and Anglican clergyman. After John Napier invented logarithms in 1614, and Edmund Gunter (1581 – 10 Dec 1626, aged 45) created the logarithmic scales (lines, or rules) upon which slide rules are based, Oughtred was the first, in 1622 (age 48), to use two such scales sliding by one another to perform direct multiplication and division (it was used for over 350 years). He also introduced the "×" symbol for multiplication, and the abbreviations "sin" and "cos" for the sine and cosine functions. He had 12 children.

- 200 years ago, in 1774, John Wilkinson, 46, (1728 – 14 July 1808, aged 80, English industrialist who pioneered the manufacture of cast iron and the use of cast-iron goods), invented a precision boring machine that could bore cast iron cylinders, such as those used in steam engines of James Watt.

- 100 years ago, in 1874, Gustave Trouvé, 35, (2 January 1839 – 27 July 1902, aged 63.5, French electrical engineer and inventor), invented the first metal detector.

Italy, Rome (753 BC), Piazza di Monte Citorio, Camera dei Deputati (back), from Via della Guglia the view of the Obelisk of Montecitorio (or Solare, 21.79 m, 33.97 m with base and globe, moved here in 1789): an ancient Egyptian red granite obelisk of Psammetichus II (595-589 BC) from Heliopolis, brought to Rome with the Flaminian obelisk in 10 BC by the Roman Emperor Augustus (63 BC – 14 AD) to be used as the gnomon (the part of a sundial that casts the shadow) of the Solarium (or Horologium) Augusti (10 BC, functioned as a giant Solar clock, built by the mathematician Facondius Novus (circa 50 BC – 15 AD).

1975 – **Galton, Cerf, Kahn**

- circa 4000 years ago, in circa 2000 BC the musical notation was invented in Sumer – the first civilization in southern Mesopotamia (now southern Iraq).

- circa 2200 years ago, in circa 225 BC the cam was invented during the Hellenistic period, used in water-driven automata.

- 1 April – 100 years ago, in 1875, Francis Galton, 53.1, prepared the first weather map published in The Times (1 April 1875, showing the weather from the previous day, 31 March), now a standard feature in newspapers worldwide.

- the microcomputer Altair 8800 was the first, and started a great development of microcomputers.

- the Internet protocol suite (commonly known as TCP/IP because the foundational protocols in the suite are the Transmission Control Protocol (TCP), and the Internet Protocol (IP)) was developed by Vinton Cerf, 32, (born 23 June 1943, age now over 75.8, American Internet pioneer, who is one of "the fathers of the Internet), and Robert E. Kahn, 37, (born 23 December 1938, age now over 80.3, American electrical engineer, who, along with Vinton Cerf, invented the Transmission Control Protocol (TCP) and the Internet Protocol (IP), the fundamental communication protocols at the heart of the Internet.) for the Defense Advanced Research Projects Agency (DARPA) ARPANET, creating the basis for the modern Internet.

.

1976 – Walker, Otto, Bell, Yagi, Uda

- circa 4000 years ago, in circa 2000 BC the chariot was invented near the Ural Mountains (now Russia).

- 150 years ago, in 1826, John Walker, 45, (29 May 1781 – 1 May 1859, aged 77.9, English inventor), invented the friction match.

- 100 years ago, in 1876, Nikolaus August Otto, 44, (14 June 1832, Holzhausen an der Haide, Nassau – 26 January 1891, aged 58.6, Cologne, German engineer who successfully developed the compressed charge internal combustion engine, which ran on petroleum gas, and led to the modern internal combustion engine - the four-stroke cycle engine.

- 100 years ago, in 1876, Alexander Graham Bell, 29, (March 3, 1847 – August 2, 1922, aged 75.4, Scottish-born American scientist, inventor, engineer, and innovator), invented and patented the first practical telephone. He also founded the American Telephone and Telegraph Company (AT&T) in 1885, at age 38. Other inventors before Bell had worked on the development of the telephone, and the invention had several pioneers.

- 19 January – Hidetsugu Yagi passed away at the age of 89.9, 9 days before 90 (28 January 1886 – 19 January 1976). He was a Japanese electrical engineer from Osaka, Japan. When working at Tohoku University 50 years ago, in 1926, he wrote several articles that introduced a new antenna designed by his younger colleague Shintaro Uda (1 June 1896 – 18 August 1976, aged 80.2) to the English-speaking world. The Yagi Antenna was widely used by the US, British, and Germans during World War II. After the war they saw extensive development as home television antennas.

Japan, Nikko, (140 km north of Tokyo, with 103 shrines and temples): a stone lantern and tall trees with ornaments, near Betsugu Taki-no-o-jinja Karamon (left, 1740, gate of the Betsugu Taki-no-o-jinja Honden (1619), part of the 23 structures of the Futarasan Shrine (1619)).

<u>1977</u> – Edison, Marrison, Horton

- circa 4000 years ago, in circa 2000 BC the glass was invented in Ancient Egypt.

- 1400 years ago, in 577, sulfur matches were invented in China.

- 100 years ago, in 1877, Thomas Edison, 30, invented the first working phonograph.

- 50 years ago, in 1927, the quartz clock was invented by Warren Marrison and J.W. Horton at Bell Telephone Laboratories.

France, Paris, mannequins representing Gustave Eiffel (right, 57 years old) talking in 1889 to Thomas Edison (left, 42 years old) in Eiffel's apartment in Tour Eiffel (1889, 324 m).

<u>1978</u> – Davy, Bell, Pelton, Fleming

- circa 3700 years ago, in circa 1700 BC the alphabet was invented in Phoenicia (now Lebanon).

- 17 December - 200th anniversary of the birth of Sir Humphry Davy (17 Dec 1778, Penzance, UK – 29 May 1829, Geneva, Switzerland, aged 50.4), Cornish chemist and inventor, who is best remembered today for isolating, using electricity, a series of elements for the first time: potassium, sodium, magnesium, calcium, strontium, boron, chlorine, iodine, and barium. In 1800 Sir Humphry Davy, 22, discovered the anesthetics properties of nitrous oxide.

- 150 years ago, in 1828, Patrick Bell, 29, (12 May 1799 – 22 April 1869, aged 69.9, Church of Scotland minister and inventor), invented the reaping machine.

- 100 years ago, in 1878, Lester Allan Pelton, 49, (5 September 1829 – 14 March 1908, aged 78.5, American inventor, who contributed significantly to the development of hydroelectricity and hydropower), invented the Pelton water wheel, at that time the most efficient design of the impulse water turbine.

- 28 September - 50 years ago, in 1928 - discovery of penicillin by Sir Alexander Fleming, 47. He gave the name penicillin on 7 March 1929, and received the Nobel Prize in 1945. The practical development of medicinal penicillin was performed by a team of medics and scientists including Howard Walter Florey, Ernst Chain and Norman Heatley.

Switzerland, 23 April 1978, Zürich (elevation 392 m – 871 m), population 400,000, on Limmat River, at the north of Zürichsee (Lake Zürich), in Bahnhofplatz. In Roman times, Turicum was a tax-collecting point at the border of Gallia Belgica (from 90 Germania Superior) and Raetia, for goods trafficked on the river Limmat. After Emperor Constantine's (272-337) reforms in 318, the border between Gaul and Italy was located east of Turicum.

<u>1979</u> – Huygens, Thimonnier, Pasteur, Swan, Edison

- circa 3500 years ago, in circa 1500 BC the seed drill was invented in Babylonia (now in Iraq, 94 km southwest of Baghdad).

- circa 2400 years ago, in circa 421 BC the crossbow (gastraphetes) and the catapult were invented in Ancient Greece (including Sicily).

- 14 April – 350th anniversary of the birth of Christaan Huygens (14 April 1629 – 8 July 1695, aged 66.2, founder of mathematical physics, had contributions in optics and mechanics, discovered Saturn's moon Titan, invented the Huygenian eyepiece for the telescope, and invented the pendulum clock in 1656, which was a breakthrough in timekeeping, and became the most accurate timekeeper for almost 300 years). It was first conceptualized in 1637 by Galileo Galilei but he was unable to create a working model.

- 150 years ago, in 1829, Barthélemy Thimonnier, 36, (19 August 1793, in L'Arbresle, Rhône – 5 July 1857, aged 63.9 in Amplepuis, French inventor) invented the first sewing machine that replicated sewing by hand.

- 100 years ago, in 1879, Louis Pasteur, 57, discovered the first vaccine, with a disease called chicken cholera. After accidentally exposing chickens to the attenuated form of a culture, he demonstrated that they became resistant to the actual virus.

- 100 years ago, in 1879, Joseph Swan, 51. and Thomas Edison, 32, both patented a functional incandescent light bulb. Some two dozen inventors had experimented with electric incandescent lighting for over 70 years, starting around 1800, but never came up with a practical design. Swan's had a low resistance, so was only suited for small installations. Edison designed a high-resistance bulb as part of a large-scale commercial electric lighting utility.

UK, London, the west front of St. Paul's Cathedral (1697, 158 m by 75 m, height 111 m, 2 towers on this side, Anglican cathedral, the seat of the Bishop of London, on Ludgate Hill, at the highest point of London, Canaletto (1697-1768), in 1746, painted The River Thames with St. Paul's Cathedral on Lord Mayor's Day), Statue of Queen Anne (1665-1714, reign 1702-1714, in 1707 England and Scotland formed Great Britain).

<u>1980</u> – Hadley, Godfrey, Budding, Zernike, Masuoka

- circa 3500 years ago, in circa 1500 BC the coins were invented in Phoenicia (now Lebanon) or Lydia (now western Turkey).

- circa 2200 years ago, in circa 220 BC the canal lock was invented in Ancient Suez Canal under Ptolemy II (283 BC – 246 BC, 37 years) in Hellenistic Egypt.

- 300 years ago, in 1680, Christaan Huygens, 51, (14 April 1629 – 8 July 1695, aged 66.2) invented the piston engine, or gunpowder engine, or explosion engine, or Huygens' engine.

- 250 years ago, in 1730, John Hadley, 48, (16 April 1682 – 14 February 1744, aged 61.8) English mathematician, invented the octant, independently of Thomas Godfrey, 26, (December 1704 – December 1749, aged 45, optician and inventor in the American colonies).

- 150 years ago, in 1830, Edwin Budding, 34, (1796 – 1846, aged 50, English engineer and inventor) invented the lawn mower, and the screw adjustable spanner (in 1842, at age 46).

- 50 years ago, in 1930, the phase-contrast microscope was invented by Frits Zernike, 42, (6 July 1888 – 10 March 1966, aged 77.7, Dutch physicist and winner of the Nobel Prize for physics in 1953 for his invention of the phase-contrast microscope).

- Flash memory, both NOR and NAND types, were invented in Japan by Fujio Masuoka, 37, (born 8 May 1943, age now over 75.9, Japanese engineer, with Ph. D. from Tohoku University), while working for Toshiba. They were introduced to the public in 1984.

Japan, Sendai, the Mathematical Institute at Tohoku University (1907), the author explaining some announcements of mathematical conferences and seminars, organized by prestigious Universities.

Japan, Sendai, Museum of Natural History at Tohoku University (founded in 1907, the third oldest Imperial University in Japan, a member of the National Seven Universities).

1981 – **Faraday, Henry, Maxwell, Benardos, Ruska**

- circa 3500 years ago, in circa 1500 BC the scissors were invented in Ancient Egypt.

- about 500 years ago, in 1481, the mariner's astrolabe was invented and used in the Portuguese circumnavigation of Africa.

- 150 years ago, in 1831, Michael Faraday, 40, (22 September 1791 – 25 August 1867, aged 75.9, British scientist who contributed to the study of electromagnetism and electrochemistry) invented a method of electromagnetic induction. It would be independently invented by Joseph Henry (17 December 1797 – 13 May 1878, aged 80.4, American mathematician and scientist who served as the first Secretary of the Smithsonian Institution, and invented the electromechanical relay in 1835) the following year, in 1832.

- 13 June - 150th anniversary of the birth of James Clerk Maxwell (13 June 1831 – 5 November 1879, aged 48.4), Scottish scientist in the field of mathematical physics), who took the work of Faraday and others and summarized it in Maxwell's equations, which are the basis of all modern theories of electromagnetic phenomena.

- 100 years ago, in 1881, Louis Pasteur, 59, developed the first vaccine for anthrax, which was used successfully in sheep, goats and cows.

- 19 April - 100 years ago, on 19 April 1881, Gustave Trouvé, 42, (after improving the efficiency of a small electric motor developed by Siemens, and using the recently developed rechargeable battery, fitted it to an English James Starley tricycle, and so inventing the world's first electric vehicle), successfully tested this vehicle along the Rue Valois in central Paris.

- - 100 years ago, in 1881, Nikolay Benardos, 39, (8 July 1842 – 21 Sep 1905, aged 63.2, Russian engineer and inventor of

Greek origin) invented the carbon arc welding, the first practical arc welding method.

    - 50 years ago, in 1931, the electron microscope was invented by Ernst Ruska, 25, (25 December 1906 – 27 May 1988, aged 81.4, German physicist who won the Nobel Prize in Physics in 1986 (age 80) for his work in electron optics, including the design of the first electron microscope).

Washington, D.C. (1790): a Lunar module in The National Air and Space Museum (1976) of the Smithsonian Institution.

1982 – Isidore, Anthemius, Hadley, Pasteur

- circa 3300 years ago, in circa 1300 BC the lathe was invented in Ancient Egypt.

- 1850 years ago, in 132, the seismometer and pendulum were invented in the Han Dynasty in China, built by Zhang Heng. It was a large metal urn-shaped instrument, which used either a suspended pendulum or an inverted pendulum acting on inertia, to dislodge a metal ball by a lever trip device.

- 1450 years ago, in 532, the pendentive dome was invented by the Greek mathematician, scientist and engineer Isidore of Miletus, 90, (442, Miletus – 537, aged 95) and mathematician Anthemius of Tralles, 58, (c. 474 – 533, aged 59) as architects, and applied for the construction (532 – 537, 5 years, using ashlar and brick) of Sancta Sophia (or Sancta Sapientia, length 82 m, width 73 m, height 55 m) in Constantinople, Eastern Roman Empire, on the orders of the Byzantine Emperor Justinian I, 50, (c. 482 – 14 Nov 565 (aged 83), reign for 38.2 years: 1 Aug 527 – 14 Nov 565). From the date of its construction in 537 until 1453, for 916 years, it served as an Eastern Orthodox cathedral and the seat of the Ecumenical Patriarch of Constantinople, except between 1204 and 1261, for 57 years, when it was converted by the Fourth Crusaders to a Roman Catholic cathedral under the Latin Empire. The building was later converted into an Ottoman mosque from 29 May 1453 until 1931, for 478 years. In 1919, the Divine Service in Sancta Sophia, which had been interrupted, after the Salvation, 466 years ago, in 1453, was continued and completed by a Greek military priest. It was then secularized and opened as a museum on 1 February 1935. It remained the world's largest cathedral for 983 years, until Seville Cathedral was completed in 1520.

- 16 April - 200th anniversary of the birth of John Hadley (16 April 1682 – 14 February 1744, aged 61.8) English mathematician, who invented the octant in 1730 (age 48), independently of Thomas Godfrey (December 1704 – December 1749, aged 45, optician and inventor in the American colonies).

- 100 years ago, in 1882, Louis Pasteur, 60, developed the first vaccine against rabies.

UK, London, from the Westminster Bridge (1862) looking southwest to the southern part of Palace of Westminster (1016, 1870, right), a tall residential building (center left) near Millbank Millennium Pier, and The Tower (left, condominium complex, on Nine Elms Lane).

Chapter 5. 1983 – 1992: Fahrenheit, Galvani, Montgolfier, Ohm, Morse, Jacobi, Hertz

<u>1983</u> – d'Abbans, Montgolfier, Armstrong

- circa 2600 years ago, in circa 600 BC the lighthouse was invented in Ancient Egypt.

- circa 2000 years ago, in circa 17 BC, the Pont-Saint-Martin (span 31.4 m) was built - a Roman segmental arch bridge in the Aosta Valley, north of Torino, in Italy, during the reign of Augustus (27 BC – 14 AD, 41 years).

- 200 years ago, in 1783, Claude-François-Dorothée, marquis de Jouffroy d'Abbans, 32, (30 September 1751 – 18 July 1832, aged 80.8) invented the steamboat. He made a paddle steamer named the Pyroscaphe ply on the Saône, river of eastern France.

- 4 June - 200 years ago, in 1783, Joseph-Michel Montgolfier, 42.8, (26 August 1740 – 26 June 1810, 69.8) and Jacques-Étienne Montgolfier, 38.5, (6 January 1745 – 2 August 1799, 54.5), who were paper manufacturers from Annonay, in Ardèche, France, invented the Montgolfière-style hot air balloon, globe aérostatique. They launched the first piloted ascent, carrying Étienne, on 4 June 1783.

- 50 years ago, in 1933, FM radio was invented by Edwin H. Armstrong, 43, (18 December 1890 – 1 February 1954, aged 63.1, American electrical engineer and inventor).

Italy, Rome (753 BC, one of the oldest cities in Europe, called Roma Aeterna (The Eternal City) and Caput Mundi (Capital of the World)), from the Pincian Hill looking southwest: Piazza del Popolo (1822), with the Egyptian obelisk (36 m) of Sety I (1290–1279 BC) and Rameses II (1303, 1279–1213 BC) from Heliopolis, brought in 10 BC by Augustus (63 BC-14 AD) for Circus Maximus, in 1589 here. Basilica San Pietro (1506, 132 m, back).

<u>1984</u> – Jacobi, Parsons

- circa 2580 years ago, in circa 580 BC the wagonway, called Diolkos, was invented and used across the Isthmus of Corinth in Ancient Greece.

- 150 years ago, in 1834, Moritz von Jacobi, 33, (21 September 1801 – 10 March 1874, aged 72.5, German-born Russian engineer and physicist, born in Potsdam, who worked mainly in Russia; he advanced progress in galvanoplastics, electric motors, and wire telegraphy; also invented electrotyping in 1838), invented the first practical electric motor. He was an older brother of the mathematician Carl Gustav Jacob Jacobi (10 December 1804 – 18 February 1851, aged 46.1, German mathematician, who made fundamental contributions to elliptic functions, dynamics, differential equations, and number theory; his name is occasionally written as Carolus Gustavus Iacobus Iacobi in his Latin books).

- 100 years ago, in 1884, Sir Charles Parsons, 30, (13 June 1854 – 11 February 1931, aged 76.6, the youngest son (the father was 54, and had 13 children) of the famous astronomer William Parsons (17 June 1800 – 31 October 1867, aged 67.3), Anglo-Irish engineer) invented the compound steam turbine.

- The first commercially available cell phone, the DynaTAC 8000X, was produced by Motorola.

Italy, Roma (753 BC, one of the oldest occupied cities in Europe, called Roma Aeterna (The Eternal City) and Caput Mundi (Capital of the World)), southeast of Piazza del Popolo (1822, by Giuseppe Valadier, inside the northern gate in the Aurelian Walls, the Porta Flaminia, now called the Porta del Popolo), near Via del Babuino (opened in 1525 as the Via Paolina) and the church Santa Maria in Montesanto (1679, begun by Rainaldi and completed by Bernini and Fontana), the statue of the Goddess of Abundance.

<u>1985</u> – Ramsden, Marum, Starley, Carothers

- circa 2570 years ago, in circa 570 BC the crank motion (rotary quern) was invented in Carthage (now northeast Tunisia and southern Spain).

- circa 2500 years ago, in 515 BC, the crane (trispastos (three-pulley-crane)) was invented in Ancient Greece.

- 6 October - 250th anniversary of the birth of Jesse Ramsden (6 October 1735 – 5 November 1800, aged 65), British mathematician, astronomical and scientific instrument maker. He invented the modern screw-cutting lathe in 1775 (age 40), and, in 1789 (age 54), he finished a 1.5 m diameter Palermo vertical circle, to measure apparent positions of astronomical objects, which was used by Giuseppe Piazzi (16 July 1746 – 22 July 1826, aged 80 years and 6 days, Italian mathematician, astronomer and Catholic priest), at the Palermo Astronomical Observatory, in constructing his catalogue of stars, and in the discovery of the dwarf planet Ceres (named by Piazzi after the Roman and Sicilian goddess of agriculture, grain crops, fertility and motherly relationship) on 1 January 1801 (at age 54.5). The great mathematician Carl Friedrich Gauss (30 April 1777 – 23 February 1855, aged 77.8) developed a new method of orbit calculation that allowed astronomers to locate Ceres again – it is the first, and largest, of the asteroids existing within the asteroid belt.

- 200 years ago, in 1785, Martinus van Marum, 35, (20 March 1750, Delft – 26 December 1837, Haarlem, aged 87.7, Dutch physician, inventor, scientist and teacher, who introduced modern chemistry in the Netherlands after the theories of Lavoisier, 42), is the first to use the electrolysis technique.

- 100 years ago, in 1885, John Kemp Starley, 31, (14 Dec 1854 – 29 Oct 1901, aged 46.8, English inventor and industrialist) invented the modern bicycle.

- 50 years ago, in 1935, nylon, the first fully synthetic fiber was produced by Wallace Carothers, 39, (27 April 1896 – 29 April 1937, aged 41 years and 2 days, American chemist, inventor and the leader of organic chemistry at DuPont).

Washington, D.C. (1790): Douglas DC-3 (1936) airplanes, at The National Air and Space Museum (1976) of the Smithsonian Institution, between Jefferson Dr SW and Independence Ave SW.

1986 – Fahrenheit, Meikle, Benz

- circa 2450 years ago, in circa 450 BC the cast iron was invented in Ancient China during the Zhou Dynasty (1122 BC – 256 BC), the oldest specimens found in a tomb of Luhe County in Jiangsu province.

- 700 years ago, in 1286, eyeglasses were invented in Italy.

- 24 May - 300th anniversary of the birth of Daniel Gabriel Fahrenheit (24 May 1686 – 16 September 1736, aged 50.3), Dutch-German-Polish physicist, inventor, and scientific instrument maker. He invented the mercury-in-glass thermometer (first practical, accurate thermometer), and Fahrenheit scale in 1709, at age 23 (first standardized temperature scale to be widely used).

- 200 years ago, in 1786, Andrew Meikle, 67, (5 May 1719 – 27 November 1811, aged 92.5, Scottish mechanical engineer) invented the threshing machine, a device used to remove the outer husks from grains of wheat. 200 years after his death, in 2011, he was one of seven inaugural inductees to the Scottish Engineering Hall of Fame.

- 100 years ago, in 1886, Karl Benz, 42, (25 November 1844 – 4 April 1929, aged 84.4, German engine designer and automobile engineer) invented the first petrol or gasoline powered auto-mobile (car).

1987 – Galilei, Galvani, Volta, Morse, Blyth

- circa 2350 years ago, in circa 350 BC, the traction trebuchet was invented in Ancient China.

- 350 years ago, in 1637, Galileo Galilei, 73, (15 February 1564 – 8 January 1642, aged 77.9) created the concept of the pendulum clock, but did not have time to create a working model.

- 250th anniversary of the birth of Luigi Aloisio Galvani (Latin: Aloysius Galvanus; 9 September 1737, Bologna, Papal States – 4 December 1798, aged 61.2, Bologna, Papal States), Italian physician, physicist, biologist and philosopher, who discovered bioelectricity. He is the pioneer of bioelectromagnetics. In 1780, he discovered that the muscles of dead frogs' legs twitched when struck by an electrical spark. Bioelectricity continues to study the electrical patterns and signals from tissues such as the nerves and muscles. After the death of Galvani, in 1799, Alessandro Volta, 54, (18 Feb 1745, Como, Duchy of Milano – 5 March 1827, Como, Lombardia-Venezia, aged 82 years and 15 days, Italian inventor) invented the battery, based on previous works by Luigi Galvani.

- 150 years ago, in 1837, Samuel Morse, 46, (27 April 1791, Charlestown, Massachusetts – 2 April 1872, New York City, aged 80.9, American painter and inventor) invented Morse code.

- 100 years ago, in 1887, James Blyth, 48, (4 April 1839 – 15 May 1906, aged 67.1, Scottish electrical engineer and academic at Anderson's College, now the University of Strathclyde, in Glasgow) invented the first wind turbine used for generating electricity.

Italy, a modern dancing girls sculpture from Pompeii (650 BC, ancient Roman town, with a complex water system, an amphitheater, gymnasium and a port, 20 km southeast of Naples, 10 km southeast of Mount Vesuvius, mostly destroyed and buried (11,000 people) under 4 to 6 m of ash and pumice in the eruption of Mount Vesuvius in 79 AD. Now there is a vast archaeological site with excavated ruins of the ancient Pompeii, and a new modern Pompei around it).

1988 – Loud, Hertz, Zuse, Hahn

- circa 2350 years ago, in circa 350 BC, the gears were invented in Ancient China.

- circa 1500 years ago, around 488, the horse collar was invented in Southern and Northern Dynasties in China.

- 100 years ago, in 1888, John J. Loud, 44, (2 November 1844 – 10 August 1916, aged 71.7, American inventor, had eight children) invented the ballpoint pen.

- 100 years ago, in 1888, Heinrich Hertz, 31, (22 February 1857 – 1 January 1894, age 36.8, German physicist) published a convincing proof of James Clerk Maxwell's (13 June 1831 – 5 November 1879, aged 48.4) electromagnetic theory of light in experiments that also demonstrate the existence of radio waves. The unit of frequency, cycle per second, was named the "Hertz" in his honor.

- 50 years ago, in 1938, the computer Z1 built by Konrad Zuse, 28, (22 June 1910 – 18 December 1995, aged 85.5, German civil engineer, inventor and computer pioneer) was the first freely programmable computer in the world.

- 50 years ago, in December 1938, nuclear fission was discovered in experiment by Otto Hahn, 59, (8 March 1879 – 28 July 1968, aged 89.3, German chemist and pioneer in the fields of radioactivity and radiochemistry, considered the father of nuclear chemistry). He was awarded the Nobel Prize in Chemistry in 1944 (age 65) for the discovery and the radiochemical proof of nuclear fission.

- 27 May - Ernst Ruska past away at the age of 81.4 (25 December 1906 – 27 May 1988) He was a German physicist who won the Nobel Prize in Physics in 1986 (age 80) for his work in electron optics, including the design of the first electron microscope 57 years ago, in 1931, at the age of 25.

France, Paris, L'Église du Dôme (1708, 107 m height, inspired by St. Peter's Basilica in Rome,1626) in the center of L'Hôtel National des Invalides (1678, founded by Louis XIV (1638–1715), in the 7th arrondissement, with military museums and monuments, and the burial site for Napoleon Bonaparte (1769-1821)). Napoleon was entombed under the Dôme of the Invalides, in a tomb made of red quartzite and resting on a green granite base, which was finished in 1861, 40 years after his death.

1989 – Lee, Lavoisier, Cartwright, Ohm, Becquerel

- 1400 years ago, in 589, the toilet paper was invented during the Sui Dynasty in China, first mentioned by the official Yan Zhitui, 58, (531 – 591, aged 60).

- 400 years ago, in 1589, the stocking frame was invented by William Lee (1563 – 1614, aged 51).

- 200 years ago, in 1789, Antoine Lavoisier, 46, discovered the law of conservation of mass, the basis for chemistry, and modern chemistry begins.

- 200 years ago, in 1789, Edmund Cartwright, 46, (24 April 1743 – 30 October 1823, aged 80.5, English inventor and clergyman, who graduated from Oxford University very early) invented the power loom.

- 16 March - 200th anniversary of the birth of Georg Simon Ohm (16 March 1789 – 6 July 1854, aged 65.3), German physicist and mathematician, who did his research with the new electrochemical cell, invented by Italian scientist Alessandro Volta. Using equipment of his own creation, Ohm found that there is a direct proportionality between the potential difference (voltage) applied across a conductor, and the resultant electric current. This relationship is known as Ohm's law.

- 150 years ago, in 1839, Edmond Becquerel, 19, (24 March 1820 – 11 May 1891, age 71.1, French physicist who studied the solar spectrum, magnetism, electricity and optics; he is also known for his work in luminescence and phosphorescence, and was the son of Antoine César Becquerel, and the father of Henri Becquerel, one of the discoverers of radioactivity), invented a method for the photovoltaic effect, thus producing the first solar cell.

France, Paris, Musée du Louvre (1793, in Palais du Louvre (1550)): from Cour Napoléon (between 1862-1867 Napoléon III reunit les Tuileries au Louvre), the right side of the central part of the western façade of Pavillon de l'Horloge or Pavillon Sully (1624 – 1654, under Kings Louis XIII (1601 – 1643, reign 1610 – 1643), and Louis XIV (1638 – 1715, reign 1643 – 1715)), which is on the east side of Cour Napoléon and of the west side of Cour Carrée.

<u>1990</u> – Swarts, Ader, Berners-Lee

- circa 2100 years ago, in circa 110 BC the paper was invented in Han Dynasty China (202 BC – 220 AD, 422 years). Some say that court eunuch Cai Lun (c. 50 – 121, aged c. 71) invented the pulp papermaking process, and established the use of new raw materials used in making paper, but ancient padding and wrapping paper artifacts dating to the 2nd century BC have been found in China.

- 100 years ago, in 1890, Frédéric Swarts, 24, (2 September 1866 – 6 September 1940, aged 74 years and 4 days, Belgian chemist) invented the first chlorofluorocarbon, $CF2Cl2$ (Freon-12), to be applied as refrigerant, as well as several other related compounds. He was a professor of civil engineering at the University of Ghent.

- 100 years ago, in 1890, Clément Ader, 49, (2 April 1841 – 3 May 1925, aged 84.1, French inventor and engineer) invented the first aircraft, or flying machine, called Eole (aircraft) or Ader Éole.

- The World Wide Web was first introduced to the public by English engineer and computer scientist Sir Tim Berners-Lee, 35, (born 8 June 1955, age now over 63.8, English engineer and computer scientist, best known as the inventor of the World Wide Web. He is currently a professor of computer science at the University of Oxford and the Massachusetts Institute of Technology (MIT). He made a proposal for an information management system on March 12, 1989, and he implemented the first successful communication between a Hypertext Transfer Protocol (HTTP) client and server via the internet in mid-November the same year.)

France, Paris, The Panthéon (1758 - 1790, 83 m height, mausoleum in the Latin Quarter in Paris, modeled on the Pantheon in Rome), seen from the west end of Rue Soufflot, near Jardin du Luxembourg (1612). This mausoleum, with the motto: *Aux grands hommes, la patrie reconnaissante* ("To the great men, the grateful homeland"), contains the remains of distinguished French citizens (Voltaire, Rousseau, Victor Hugo, etc.). In 1851, physicist Léon Foucault demonstrated the rotation of the earth by his experiment conducted in the Panthéon, by constructing a 67 m Foucault pendulum beneath the central dome.

1991 – Faraday, Judson, Bardeen

- 2200 years ago, in 209 BC, the Terracotta Warriors were created - terracotta sculptures depicting the armies of Qin Shi Huang, the first Emperor of China. It was a form of funerary ceremony, buried with the emperor in 210 BC – 209 BC.

- 1700 years ago, in circa 291, the crank and connecting rod (Roman Hierapolis sawmill) was invented by Romans in Asia Minor, Roman Empire.

- 550 years ago, in 1441, the water gauge was invented in Korea.

- 200th anniversary of the birth of Michael Faraday (22 September 1791 – 25 August 1867, aged 75.9), British scientist who contributed to the study of electromagnetism and electrochemistry. His main discoveries include the principles underlying electromagnetic induction, diamagnetism and electrolysis. James Clerk Maxwell (13 June 1831 – 5 November 1879, aged 48.4), Scottish scientist in the field of mathematical physics) took the work of Faraday and others and summarized it in Maxwell's equations, which are the basis of all modern theories of electromagnetic phenomena.

- 100 years ago, in 1891, Whitcomb Judson, 45, (15 March 1846 – 8 December 1909, aged 63.7, American mechanical engineer and inventor) invented the zipper.

- 30 January - John Bardeen passed away at the age of 82.7 (23 May 1908 – 30 January 1991, Boston, Mass). He was an American physicist and electrical engineer, and is the only person to be awarded the Nobel Prize in Physics twice: first in 1956 (age 48) with William Shockley and Walter Brattain for the invention of the transistor in December 1947 (age 39), and again in 1972 (age 64) with Leon N. Cooper and John Robert Schrieffer, for a fundamental theory of conventional superconductivity known as the BCS theory.

Italy, il Campanile del Santuario de la Santissima Vergine del Rosario (Cordi Iesu Sacrum, Anno Iubilaei 1925), in the downtown of the modern Pompei (650 BC, ancient Roman town with a complex water system, an amphitheater, gymnasium and a port, 20 km southeast of Naples, 10 km southeast of Mount Vesuvius, mostly destroyed and buried (11,000 people) under 4 to 6 m of ash and pumice in the eruption of Mount Vesuvius in 79 AD. Now there is a vast archaeological site with excavated ruins of the ancient Pompeii, and a new modern Pompei around it).

1992 – Song, Pascal, Musschenbroek, Chappe, Lawes, Bouly

- 1700 years ago, in circa 292, the turbine was invented by Romans in the Africa Province of the Roman Empire.

- about 900 years ago, around 1092, the endless power-transmitting chain drive was invented by Su Song, 72, (1020 – 1101, aged 81, mathematician, astronomer, engineer, and ambassador of the Song Dynasty from China), for the development of an astronomical clock (the Cosmic Engine).

- 350 years ago, in 1642, Blaise Pascal, 21, invented the Pascaline or mechanical calculator.

- 14 March - 300th anniversary of the birth of Pieter van Musschenbroek (14 March 1692 – 19 September 1761, aged 69.5), Dutch scientist, professor in Duisburg, Utrecht, and Leiden, in mathematics, philosophy, medicine, and astronomy. He invented the first capacitor in 1746 (age 54):

- 200 years ago, in 1792, Claude Chappe, 29, (25 December 1763 – 23 January 1805, aged 41, French engineer and inventor) demonstrated a practical semaphore telegraph system - the first messages were successfully sent between Paris and Lille (200 km northeast of Paris); this system eventually spanned all of France. His system consisted of a series of towers, each within line of sight of others, each supporting a wooden mast with two crossarms on pivots that could be placed in various positions. The operator in a tower moved the arms to a sequence of positions, spelling out text messages in semaphore code. The operator in the next tower read the message through a telescope, then passed it on to the next tower. This was the first practical telecommunications system of the industrial age, and was used for 60 years, until 1852, when electric telegraph systems replaced it. The Chappe semaphore figures prominently in Alexandre Dumas' (24 July 1802 – 5 December 1870, aged 68.3, also known as Alexandre Dumas père (French for 'father'), French writer (*Les Trois Mousquetaires* (The Three

Musketeers) 1844 (age 42)) The Count of Monte Cristo (1844, age 42). The Count bribes an underpaid operator to transmit a false message.

- 150 years ago, in 1842, John Bennet Lawes, 28, (28 December 1814 – 31 August 1900, aged 85.6, English entrepreneur and agricultural scientist, who founded an experimental farm at his home at Rothamsted Manor that eventually became the Rothamsted Experimental Station, the oldest agricultural research facility in the world), developed a superphosphate, the first man-made fertilizer, that would mark the beginnings of the chemical fertilizer industry.

- 100 years ago, in 1892, Léon Bouly, 20, (1872–1932, aged 60, French inventor) invented the word and device cinematograph.

UK, London, from the west end of Westminster Bridge (1862) looking northwest to a horse bronze statue (1883, erected 1902) with Boadicea (circa 10 – 61) on a Roman chariot, by Thomas Thornycroff (1815-1885).

Paris, A statue by Aristide Maillol (1861 – 1944) in Jardin des Tuileries (created in 1564 as the garden of Palais des Tuileries (1564 – 1883, which was located between le Pavillion de Marsan (right), at the west end of the north part of Musée du Louvre, and Pavillon de Flore, at the west end of the south part of Musée du Louvre)).

Chapter 6. 1993 – 2002: Gutenberg, Celsius, Röntgen, Diesel, Marconi

<u>1993</u> – Galilei, Whitney, Diesel

- 400 years ago, in 1593, Galileo Galilei, 29, invented the thermometer.

- 200 years ago, in 1793, Eli Whitney, 28, (8 December 1765, Westborough, Massachusetts, British America – 8 January 1825, New Haven, Connecticut, U.S.A., aged 59 years and 1 month, American engineer and inventor, had 4 children) invented the modern cotton gin.

- 100 years ago, in 1893, Rudolf Diesel, 35, (18 March 1858, Paris, France – 29 September 1913, aged 55.5, German inventor and mechanical engineer) invented the diesel engine (also Herbert Akroyd Stuart (28 January 1864, Halifax, Yorkshire, England – 19 February 1927, Halifax, 63, English inventor who invented the hot bulb engine, or heavy oil engine) had experimented with compression ignition before Diesel).

- Mosaic, the first popular web browser was introduced.

Paris, La Monnaie de Paris (the Direction of Coins and Medals) created in 864 by Charles II (823-877, king 843-877), is the oldest French institution, which is still active. It also has a Musée de la Monnaie (1833), at 11 Quai de Conti, in the 6th arrondissement.

1994 – Davis

- Circa 1500 years ago, around 494, the pointed arch bridge, or Karamagara Bridge, was first built by the Romans in Cappadocia, Eastern Roman Empire.

- 400 years ago, in 1594, the backstaff was invented by Captain John Davis (c. 1550 – 29 Dec 1605, aged 55).

- October - Stanford Federal Credit Union in Palo Alto, California, becomes the first financial institution to offer online internet banking services to all of its members.

UK, London, from Parliament Square, looking southwest to the Church of St Margaret of Antioch (1523, the Anglican parish church of the House of Commons), 20 m northeast of the Westminster Abbey.

1995 – Bramah, Marconi, Röntgen

- 200 years ago, in 1795, Joseph Bramah, 47, (13 April 1748 – 9 December 1814, aged 66.6, English inventor) invented the hydraulic press.

- 100 years ago, in 1895, Guglielmo Marconi, 21, (25 April 1874 – 20 July 1937, aged 63.2, Italian inventor and electrical engineer, worked on long-distance radio transmission, discovered Marconi's law and a radio telegraph system, invented radio, and he shared the 1909 Nobel Prize in Physics with Karl Ferdinand Braun "in recognition of their contributions to the development of wireless telegraphy") invented a system of wireless communication using radio waves.

- 8 November - 100 years ago, on 8 November 1895, Wilhelm Röntgen, 50.6, (27 March 1845, Lennep, Prussia (now Remscheid, Germany) – 10 Feb 1923, Munich, Germany, aged 77.9, German mechanical engineer and physicist) produced and detected electromagnetic radiation in a wavelength range known as X-rays or Röntgen rays (or radiograph), which became important in medical diagnosis and therapy, an achievement that earned him the first Nobel Prize in Physics in 1901, at age 56.

- DVD (Digital Versatile Disc, an optical disc storage format) was invented and developed by Philips, Sony, Toshiba, and Panasonic. DVDs offer higher storage capacity than Compact Discs (CDs), while having the same dimensions.

USA, UC Berkeley (1868, motto Fiat lux), from Campanile (1914, 94 m) looking north-northwest: Mathematics Dep. and Economics Dep. (right middle), Civil Engineering Dep. (next back), Nanofabrication Lab. (next back), Transportation Inst. (center left), Earth Sciences and Map Library and Seismological Lab (next left), Graduate School of Journalism (next back), Center for Developing Economies (next right), Memorial Glade (green center left).

1996 – **Jenner, Senefelder**

- about 1000 years ago, in 996, the fire lance was invented during the Song Dynasty (960 – 1279, for 319 years) in China, with a tube of first bamboo, and later of metal, that shot a weak gunpowder blast of flame and shrapnel.

- 14 May – 200 years ago, in 1796, Edward Jenner, 46.99, (17 May 1749 – 26 Jan 1823, aged 73.6, English physician and scientist) administered the first smallpox vaccination; smallpox killed an estimated 400,000 Europeans each year during the 18th century, including five reigning monarchs.

- 200 years ago, in 1796, Alois Senefelder, 25, (6 November 1771 – 26 February 1834, aged 62.3, German engineer, actor and playwright) invented the lithography printing technique.

UK, Oxford, a Public Library close to Christ Church College (1546) and Merton College (1264, named after Walter de Merton).

<u>1997</u> – Stopler, Bentham

- about 1000 years ago, in 997, the fireworks were invented during the Song Dynasty (960 – 1279, for 319 years) in China, in the early age of gunpowder. Fireworks could be purchased from market vendors; these were made of sticks of bamboo packed with gunpowder.

- 400 years ago, in 1597, the revolver was invented by Hans Stopler.

- 200 years ago, in 1797, Samuel Bentham, 40, (11 January 1757 – 31 May 1831, aged 74.3, English mechanical engineer, inventor and naval architect, moved to Russia for 13 years, and to France for 12 years, had 4 children) invented plywood.

UK, Cambridge, From the entrance on Queens' Ln, looking west to Queens' College (1448, by Margaret of Anjou (1430-1482)) Old Court (1448-1451).

The north-west and south-west sides of the Tour Eiffel (1889, 324 m) with the north (pilier nord, left, has an elevator (1986)), west (center) and south (right) legs. Work on the foundations started on 28 January 1887. Those for the east and south (right) legs had each leg resting on four 2 m concrete slabs; for the other two, each slab has two piles 15 m long and 6 m in diameter, to a depth of 22 m to support the concrete slabs 6 m thick.

<u>1998</u> – Gutenberg, Pechmann

- 600th anniversary of the birth of Johannes Gensfleisch zur Laden zum Gutenberg (1398 – 3 February 1468, aged 69), known as Gutenberg, German blacksmith, goldsmith, printer, and publisher, who introduced printing to Europe with the printing press, in 1439, at age 41, in Mainz, Holy Roman Empire, now Germany.

- 100 years ago, in 1898, Hans von Pechmann, 48, (1 April 1850 – 19 April 1902, aged 52, German chemist, discovered diazomethane in 1894 (age 44), Pechmann condensation, Pechmann pyrazole synthesis, prepared 1,2-diketones (e.g., diacetyl), acetonedicarboxylic acid, methylglyoxal, diphenyltriketone, and established the symmetrical structure of anthraquinone) produced the first example of solid polyethylene serendipitously, via the decomposition of diazomethane. He studied with Heinrich Limpricht at the University of Greifswald, and became Professor at the University of Munich until 1895 (age 45); them he was professor at the University of Tübingen for 7 years, from 1895 until 1902. Polyethylene is now the most common plastic in the world.

Italy, Rome (753 BC), Piazza Colonna, the northwest side of The Doric Column (193, 40 m, 27 blocks of Carrara marble, diameter 3.78 m, stairway of 200 steps within) of Marcus Aurelius (Latin: *Columna Centenaria Divorum Marci et Faustinae*), with a spiral relief: it was built in honor of Roman emperor and one of the most important Stoic philosophers Marcus Aurelius (121 – 180, joint 16th emperor 161 – 180, regarding the triumph over the Marcomanni, Quadi and Sarmatians in the year 176), and modeled on Trajan's Column. (113, 35 m, Traianus (53–117)).

1999 – **Volta, Robert, Medhurst, Jungner**

- about 1000 years ago, around 999, the drydocks were invented during the Song Dynasty (960 – 1279, for 319 years) in China.

- 200 years ago, in 1799, Alessandro Volta, 54, (18 Feb 1745, Como, Duchy of Milano – 5 March 1827, Como, Lombardia-Venezia, aged 82 years and 15 days, Italian inventor) invented the battery, based on previous works by Luigi Galvani (9 September 1737 – 4 December 1798, aged 61.2).

- 200 years ago, in 1799, Louis-Nicolas Robert, 38, (2 December 1761 – 8 August 1828, aged 66.6, French mechanical engineer) invented the first paper-making machine that became the blueprint of the Fourdrinier (brothers Henry (11 February 1766 – 3 September 1854, aged 88.5), and 7.6 years younger Sealy (9 October 1773 – 1847, aged 74)) machine.

- 200 years ago, in 1799, George Medhurst, 40, (1759 – 1827, aged 68, English mechanical engineer and inventor) invented the first motorized air compressor.

- 100 years ago, in 1899, Waldemar Jungner, 30, (June 19, 1869 – August 30, 1924 (of pneumonia), 55.2, Swedish inventor and engineer) invented the nickel-iron electric storage battery (NiFe), the nickel-cadmium battery (NiCd), and the rechargeable alkaline silver-cadmium battery (AgCd). As an inventor he also fabricated a fire alarm based on different dilutions of metals. He worked on the electrolytic production of sodium carbonate, and patented a rock drilling device.

Italy, Rome (753 BC, one of the oldest cities in Europe, called Roma Aeterna (The Eternal City) and Caput Mundi (Capital of the World)), in Villa Borghese (1630), Arco di Settimio Severo (1750, Septimius Severus (born 145, reign 193 – 211), his predecessor was the 19th Emperor of the Roman Empire, Didius Julianus (born 133, reign 28 March 193 – 1 June 193).

<u>2000</u> – Cristofori, Kober

- about 1000 years ago, around 1000, the ambulance was invented by the Crusaders, east of the Mediterranean Sea (now Lebanon and Palestine).

- about 300 years ago, in 1700, Bartolomeo Cristofori di Francesco, 45, (4 May 1655 – 27 Jan 1731, aged 75.7) invented the piano, at the request of the Grand Prince Ferdinando de' Medici, 37, (9 Aug 1663 in Palazzo Pitti, Firenze, Toscana – 31 Oct 1713 in the same Palazzo Pitti, aged 50.2), who hired Cristofori (age 33) in 1688.

- 100 years ago, in 1900, Theodor Kober, 35, (13 February 1865, Stuttgart - 20 December 1930, Friedrichshafen, aged 65.8, German aviation engineer) designed the first Zeppelin (named after Ferdinand Adolf Heinrich August Graf von Zeppelin (8 July 1838 – 8 March 1917, aged 78 years and 8 months), German general and later inventor of the Zeppelin rigid airships; he founded the company Luftschiffbau Zeppelin).

<u>2001</u> – Celsius, Booth, Kenney

- 2001 is the 1st year of the 3rd millennium, and the 1st year of the 21st century.

- 27 November – 300th anniversary of the birth of Anders Celsius (27 November 1701 – 25 April 1744, aged 42.4), Swedish mathematician, astronomer, and physicist. He founded the Uppsala Astronomical Observatory in 1741, and in 1742 proposed the Celsius temperature scale, which bears his name.

- 100 years ago, in 1901, independently British engineer Hubert Cecil Booth, 30, (4 July 1871 – 14 January 1955, aged 83.5) and American inventor David T. Kenney, 35, (3 April 1866 – 26 May 1922, aged 56.1) invented the first motorized cleaner using suction, a powered "vacuum cleaner".

UK, Oxford, University of Oxford, School of Anthropology and Museum Ethnography, Institute of Social and Cultural Anthropology, at 51 - 53 Banbury Road.

East of Louvre: Place du Louvre, the north tower (1860, with a bell called "Marie", center) of l'Église Saint-Germain l'Auxerrois (founded around 650, rebuilt many times, with a porch which has a rose window, and a balustrade above which encircles the whole church, from 1439, right), and la Mairie du 1er Arrondissment (1859, left). Inside the church are a 15th-century wooden statue of Saint Germain, and a stone carved statue of Saint-Vincent.

2002 – Guericke, Davy, Carrier

- 20 November - 400th anniversary of the birth of Otto von Guericke (20 November 1602 – 11 May, 1686, aged 83.5 (Julian calendar); 30 November 1602 – 21 May 1686 (Gregorian calendar, introduced on Thursday, 4 October 1582, which was followed by the first day of the Gregorian calendar, Friday, 15 October 1582, but each country adopted the Gregorian calendar at different times (Prussia 28 years later , in 1610, the British Empire, including the current U.S., 170 years later, in 1752)), German scientist, inventor, and politician. He developed the physics of vacuums in 1650 (age 48), and demonstrated electrostatic repulsion with his friction machine in 1663 (age 61).

- 200 years ago, in 1802, Humphry Davy, 24, invented the arc lamp (to work well, needed good electric generators). Davy, 35, appointed Michael Faraday, 22, as Chemical Assistant at the Royal Institution on 1 March 1813.

- 100 years ago, in 1902, Willis Carrier, 26, invents the first modern electrical air conditioning unit.

Chapter 7. 2003 – 2012: Heron, Mercator, Franklin

2003 – Gorrie, Elling, Bénédictus, Wright

- 400 years ago, in 1603, Accademia Nazionale dei Lincei was founded in Rome, Italy (the author was invited here in 1977).

- 3 October - 200th anniversary of the birth of John Gorrie (3 October 1803 – 29 June 1855, aged 51.7), American physician, scientist, and inventor of mechanical cooling.

- 100 years ago, in 1903, Ægidius Elling, 42, (26 July 1861 – 27 May 1949, aged 87.8, Norwegian researcher, inventor and pioneer of gas turbine, who is considered to be the father of the gas turbine) built the first gas turbine that was able to produce more power than needed to run its own components.

- 100 years ago, in 1903, Édouard Bénédictus, 25, (1878 - 28 Jan 1930, aged 52, French painter and chemist) discovered laminated glass.

- 100 years ago, in 1903, the Wright Brothers Wilbur, 36, (April 16, 1867 – May 30, 1912, aged 45), and Orville, 32, (August 19, 1871 – January 30, 1948, aged 76.5), discovered how to fly with first manually controlled, fixed wing, motorized aircraft, at Kitty Hawk, North Carolina.

Washington, D.C. (1790): the 1903 Wright Flyer airplane, at The National Air and Space Museum (1976) of the Smithsonian Institution, between Jefferson Dr SW and Independence Ave SW.

2004 – Trevithick, Sertüner, Seishū, Fleming

- about 600 years ago, in 1404, the coil spring was invented in Europe.

- 21 February - 200 years ago, in 1804, Richard Trevithick, 32.9, (13 April 1771 – 22 April 1833, aged 62 years and 9 days, British inventor and mining engineer), invented the steam locomotive, and he world's first locomotive-hauled railway journey took place on 21 February 1804.

- 200 years ago, in 1804, Friedrich Wilhelm Adam Sertüner, 21, (19 June 1783 – 20 February 1841, aged 57.6, German pharmacist and a pioneer of Alkaloid chemistry) discovered morphine as the first active alkaloid extracted from the opium poppy plant.

- 200 years ago, in 1804, Hanaoka Seishū, 44, (23 October 1760 – 21 November 1835, aged 75, Japanese surgeon of the Edo period, with a knowledge of Chinese herbal medicine, as well as Western surgical techniques he had learned through Rangaku (literally "Dutch learning", or "Western learning")), was the first to perform surgery using general anesthesia - he created tsūsensan, the first modern general anesthetic.

- 100 years ago, in 1904, the Fleming valve, the first vacuum tube and diode, was invented by John Ambrose Fleming, 55, (29 November 1849 – 18 April 1945, aged 95.4, English electrical engineer and physicist, who invented the first thermionic valve or vacuum tube, designed the radio transmitter with which the first transatlantic radio transmission was made, and also established the right-hand rule used in physics).

Japan: the five-storied pagoda Gojunoto (1818, which has at the top the same altitude like the height of Tokyo Skytree (2011), 634 m) in Nikkō (140 km north of Tokyo, 25 km west of Utsunomiya, the capital of Tochigi Prefecture) - a town at the entrance to Nikko National Park, in the mountains (600 m) of Tochigi Prefecture, most famous for Toshogu, Japan's most lavishly decorated shrine, and the mausoleum of Tokugawa Ieyasu, the founder of the Tokugawa shogunate (1600).

2005 – Carolus

- about 800 years ago, in 1205, the earliest form of mechanical escapement, the verge escapement, was invented in Europe.

- 400 years ago, in 1605, the first newspaper called "Relation aller Fürnemmen und gedenckwürdigen Historien" (Account of all distinguished and commemorable news) was published by Johann Carolus, 30, (1575 – 1634, aged 59) in Strasburg, Holy Roman Empire of the German Nation.

Germany - 23 March 1978, Freibourg im Breisgau (1120 by Duke Berthold III of Zähringen (1085-1122), elevation 278 m, the south façade of Freiburger Münster (cathedral, 1200, 116 m, J. S. Bach (1685-1750) performed here).

2006 – **Franklin**

- 17 January – 300th anniversary of the birth of Benjamin Franklin (January 17, 1706 – April 17, 1790, aged 84 years and 3 months), an American polymath and one of the Founding Fathers of the United States. Franklin was a leading author, printer, political theorist, politician, freemason, postmaster, scientist, inventor, humorist, civic activist, statesman, and diplomat. As a scientist he is known for his discoveries and theories regarding electricity. As an inventor, he is known for the lightning rod, bifocals (very useful for medical applications), and the Franklin stove, among other inventions. He founded many civic organizations, including Philadelphia's fire department and the University of Pennsylvania.

USA, Boston: a view of the north-east part of Boston, from Cambridge, over Charles River Basin. Federal Reserve Bank Building (187 m, left), and other tall buildings in the financial district.

2007 – Niépce, Rivaz, Fulton, Cornu

- about 600 years ago, in 1407, the mainspring was invented in Europe.

- 200 years ago, in 1807, Joseph Nicéphore Niépce, 42, (7 March 1765 – 5 July 1833, aged 68.3, or Nicéphore Niépce, French inventor, who invented photography, developed heliography in 1822 (age 57), a technique he used to create the world's oldest surviving product of a photographic process: a print made from a photoengraved printing plate in 1825. In 1826 or 1827, he used a primitive camera to produce the oldest surviving photograph of a real-world scene. Among Niépce's other inventions was the Pyréolophore, the world's first internal combustion engine capable of doing useful work, which he conceived, created, and developed with his older brother Claude in 1807.

- 200 years ago, in 1807, François Isaac de Rivaz (19 December 1752, Paris – 30 July 1828, Sion, Switzerland, aged 75.6, inventor and Swiss politician), invented a hydrogen-powered internal combustion engine with electric ignition, and described it in a French patent published in 1807. In 1808 he fitted it into a primitive working vehicle – the world's first internal combustion powered automobile. In 1824, the French physicist Nicolas Léonard Sadi Carnot scientifically established the thermodynamic theory of idealized heat engines. Gasoline was not used for internal combustion engines until 1870, when carburetors were invented, to convert non-combustible liquid fuels into a combustible gaseous mixture form.

- 200 years ago, in 1807, Robert Fulton (1765 – 1815, aged 49.2) launched, when he was 42, the first commercially successful steamboat that brought passengers from New York to Albany in 1807. Born in the same year as Fulton, Eli Whitney (1765 - 1825, aged 59 years and 1 month) created, when he was 28, the mechanical cotton gin in 1793.

- 13 November - 100 years ago, on 13 Nov 1907, the first free flight of a rotary-wing aircraft (helicopter) was carried out by Paul Cornu, 26, (15 June 1881 – 6 June 1944, aged 62.9, French engineer).

USA, July 1980, from New York Harbor looking northeast to the southwest sides of the Statue of Liberty and twin towers (1973-2001, 417 m and 415 m, 3.3 km away).

<u>2008</u> – Torricelli, Ford, Brandenberger

- about 600 years ago, in 1407, the rifle was invented in Europe.

- 15 October – 400th anniversary of the birth of Evangelista Torricelli (15 October 1608 – 25 October 1647, aged 39 years and 10 days), Italian mathematician and physicist, best known for his invention of the barometer in 1643 (age 35), his advances in optics, and work on the method of indivisibles.

- 100 years ago, in 1908, Henry Ford, 45, (July 30, 1863 – April 7, 1947, aged 83.6) developed the first mass produced automobile, the Model T, and designed to put average Americans in his cars.

- 100 years ago, in 1908, cellophane was invented by Jacques E. Brandenberger, 36, (19 October 1872 – 13 July 1954, aged 81.7, Swiss chemist and textile engineer).

France, Paris, A statue by Aristide Maillol (1861 – 1944) in Jardin du Carrousel, which is the eastern part of Jardin des Tuileries (created in 1564 as the garden of Palais des Tuileries (1564 – 1883, which was located between le Pavillion de Marsan (back, with the entrance to Les Arts Décoratifs), at the west end of the north part of Musée du Louvre, and Pavillon de Flore, at the west end of the south part of Musée du Louvre)).

<u>2009</u> – Fahrenheit, Rignoux, Fournier

- 300 years ago, in 1709, Daniel Gabriel Fahrenheit, 23, (24 May 1686 – 16 September 1736, aged 50.3), Dutch-German-Polish physicist, inventor, and scientific instrument maker, invented the mercury-in-glass thermometer (first practical, accurate thermometer), and Fahrenheit scale (first standardized temperature scale, based on alcohol freezing point, to be widely used).

- 100 years ago, in 1909, the first instantaneous transmission of images, or television broadcast, was carried out in Paris by the Frenchmen Georges Rignoux and Professor A. Fournier.

Switzerland, Geneva, the Monument (1879) for Charles II, Duke of Brunswick (30 Oct 1804 in Brunswick (Braunschweig), Germany-19 August 1873, aged 68.8 (died in Geneva at Beau Rivage Hotel), ruled the Duchy of Brunswick 1815-1830).

2010 – Heron, Appert, Koenig, Cugnot

- 2000th anniversary of the birth of Heron of Alexandria (c. 10 AD – c. 70 AD, aged circa 60), mathematician and engineer, who was active in his native city of Alexandria, Roman Egypt. He is considered the greatest experimenter of antiquity. Hero published a description of a steam-powered device called an aeolipile (or "Heron engine"). Among his most famous inventions was a windwheel, constituting the earliest instance of wind harnessing on land. A windwheel operating an organ was the first instance in history of wind powering a machine. The first vending machine was also one of his inventions, as well as automatic doors.

- 200 years ago, in 1810, Nicolas Appert, 61, (17 November 1749, Châlons-sur-Marne (present Châlons-en-Champagne), present Marne, France – 1 June 1841, Massy, France, aged 91.5, confectioner and French inventor) invented the airtight food preservation, and he is known as the father of canning. Appert published a book (200 copies) describing his process in 1810, entitled "L'Art de conserver les substances animales et végétales" (The Art of Preserving Animal and Vegetable Substances). This was the first cookbook of its kind on modern food preservation methods.

- 200 years ago, in 1810, Friedrich Koenig, 36, (17 April 1774 – 17 January 1833, aged 58.7, German inventor) received in London a patent on his high-speed steam-powered printing press with a cylinder, which he built together with watchmaker Andreas Friedrich Bauer. This new style of printing press could print up to 1,100 sheets per hour, printing on both sides of the paper at the same time; first trial run was in April 1812. The first issue of The Times, printed with the new presses, was published on 29 November 1814.

- This year, 241 years after Nicolas-Joseph Cugnot, in 1769, built his first automobile or "fardier de Cugnot", a copy of the "fardier de Cugnot" was built by pupils at the Arts et Métiers ParisTech, a French Grande école, and the city of Void-Vacon. This replica worked perfectly, proving that the concept was viable and verifying the truth and results of the 1769 tests. This replica was exhibited at the 2010 Paris Motor Show. It is now exhibited in Cugnot's native village of Void-Vacon, France.

Germany, 23 March 1978, looking west to Neuenburg am Rhein (440 km southwest of Göttingen), near the border with France, Mulheim ahead (west), Breisach left (north), Schliengen right (south).

2011 – **Wilson**

- about 800 years ago, in 1211, the familiar mariner's dry compass, which uses a pivoting needle suspended above a compass-card in a glass box, was invented in medieval Europe.

- 100 years ago, in 1911, the cloud chamber, the first particle detector, was invented by Charles Thomson Rees Wilson, 42, (14 February 1869 – 15 November 1959, aged 90.7, Scottish physicist and meteorologist, who won the Nobel Prize in Physics, in 1927, for his invention of the cloud chamber).

Tokyo, the Skytree (2011, 634 m, a broadcasting, restaurant, and observation tower located in Sumida, north of Asakusa Dori).

<u>2012</u> – Mercator, Newcomen, Clanny

- about 1200 years ago, in 812, the number zero appeared in Ancient India.

- 5 March – 500th anniversary of the birth of Gerardus Mercator (5 March 1512 – 2 December 1594, aged 82.6), Southern Dutch (current day Belgium) cartographer, geographer and cosmographer. He was renowned for creating the 1569 (age 57) world map based on a cylindrical projection (Mercator projection), which represented sailing courses of constant bearing (rhumb lines) as straight lines—an innovation that is still used in nautical charts. He also invented the term Atlas. He had six children.

- 300 years ago, in 1712, Thomas Newcomen, 48, (February 1664 – 5 August 1729, aged 65.5, English inventor) invented the atmospheric engine, the first practical fuel-burning engine, and the first commercial steam engine to pump water out of mines. Newcomen's engine, unlike Thomas Savery's, 62, (c. 1650 – 1715, aged 65, English inventor) engine of 1698, uses a piston.

- 200 years ago, in 1812, William Reid Clanny, 36, (1776 – 10 January 1850, aged 74, Irish physician and inventor) invented a safety lamp, which he improved in later years. Safety lamps based on Clanny's improved design were used until the adoption of electric lamps, about 100 years later.

Chapter 8. 2013 – 2019: Mendeleev, Armstrong

2013 – Archimedes, Bergius

- 2300th anniversary of the birth of Archimedes (c. 287 BC Syracuse, Sicily, Magna Graecia – c. 212 BC Syracuse, Sicily, Magna Graecia), Greek mathematician, physicist, engineer, inventor, and astronomer. He invented Archimedes' screw.

- 100 years ago, in 1913, the Bergius process, for producing synthetic fuel from coal, was developed by Friedrich Bergius, 29, (11 October 1884, near Breslau (now Wrocław, Poland), within the German Empire's Prussian Province of Silesia – 30 March 1949, Buenos Aires, Argentina, aged 64.5), German chemist, received the Nobel Prize in Chemistry (1931, together with Carl Bosch) in recognition of contributions to the invention and development of chemical high-pressure methods. After WWII he moved to Argentina, where he acted as adviser to the Ministry of Industry.

<u>2014</u> – Napier, Armstrong

About 1600 years ago, in 414, the paddle wheel boat, described in the anonymous book "De rebus bellicis", was invented by the Romans in the Roman Empire.

- 400 years ago, in 1614, John Napier, 64, (1550 – 4 April 1617, aged 67; Scottish mathematician, physicist, and astronomer. His Latinized name was Ioannes Neper) published Mirifici Logarithmorum Canonis Descriptio, the first table of logarithms.

- 100 years ago, in 1914, Edwin Armstrong, 24, (18 December 1890 – 1 February 1954, aged 63.1, American electrical engineer and inventor)., invented and patented the regenerative circuit.

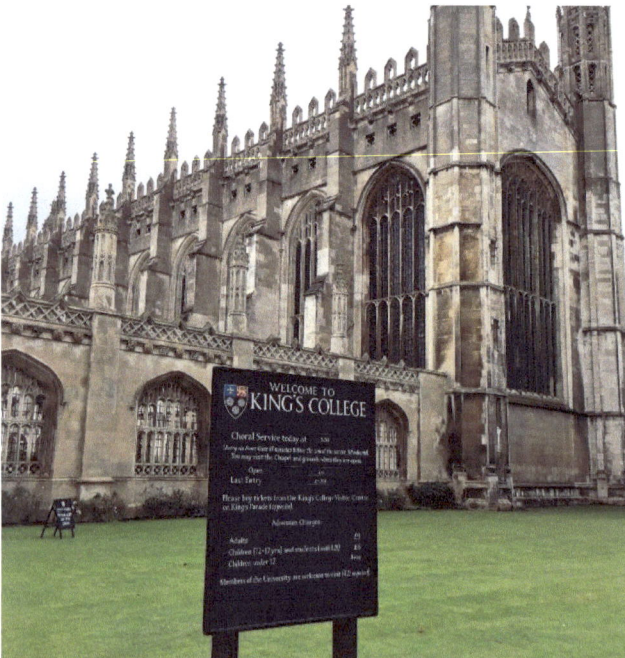

UK, Cambridge, from the entrance to King's College (1441), looking northwest to the Chapel (the south façade (center left), and the east façade (right)).

<u>2015</u> – Franklin, Carson

- 300 years ago, in 1715, Benjamin Franklin was 9, and had his final formal year of schooling, at Boston Latin School.

USA, Boston, 3 Dec 2009, from Avenue Louis Pasteur (1822-1895, French microbiologist), Boston Public Latin School (1635, Schola Latina Bostoniensis, the oldest and the first public exam school in the U.S.).

- 100 years ago, in 1915, John Renshaw Carson, 29, (28 June 1886 – 31 October 1940, aged 54.3, noted transmission theorist) invented SBB (Single-Sideband Modulation).

<u>2016</u> – Stirling

- about 1200 years ago, around 816, the algebra appeared east of the Mediterranean Sea (now Syria).

- 200 years ago, in 1816, Robert Stirling, 26, (25 October 1790 – 6 June 1878, aged 87.6, had 7 children, Scottish clergyman, and inventor) invented, with his younger brother James Stirling, the Stirling engine. Though the Stirling engine is rarely used today, its apparently perpetual motion capability continues to draw the interest of research institutions like Los Alamos National Laboratory and NASA. On 3 October 2014 Stirling was inducted into the Scottish Engineering Hall of Fame.

Washington, D.C. (1790): a vending cart near the east side of the Smithsonian Institution Building (1849-1855), on Jefferson Drive SW, close to 7th Street SW.

2017 – Drais

- about 1200 years ago, around 817, the gunpowder was invented during the Tang Dynasty in China, by Chinese alchemists searching for an elixir of immortality. Evidence of gunpowder's first use in China comes from the Five Dynasties (Tang is one of them) and Ten Kingdoms period (618 – 907, for 289 years). The earliest known recorded recipes for gunpowder are written in a military manuscript compiled in 1044, during the Song Dynasty (960 – 1279, for 319 years).

- 12 June - 200 years ago, on 12 June 1817, Baron Karl von Drais, 32, (29 April 1785, in Karlsruhe – 10 December 1851, in Karlsruhe, aged 66.6, German forest official and inventor) invented the Laufmaschine (running machine, called also draisine), an early velocipede and precursor to the modern bicycle, with his first ride of 7 km in Mannheim, on 12 June 1817.

Japan, north-west of the Sendai Station (1887), on Ekimae Dori, the restaurant Rigoletto, named after the famous opera with the same name, by Giuseppe Verdi (1813 – 1901), who wrote 37 operas, Rigoletto being the 17th, with the premiere at Teatro La Fenice, Venezia, on 11 March 1851.

2018 – Brunel, Armstrong

- 1900 years ago, in 118, the wheelbarrow was invented in China, and it was found in a tomb at Chengdu, Sichuan province, from the Han Dynasty period in China.

- 200 years ago, in 1818, Marc Isambard Brunel, 49, (25 April 1769 – 12 December 1849, aged 80.6, French-born engineer who settled in England) invented the tunneling shield, and constructed the Thames Tunnel. He also worked many projects in the U.S.A., and in 1796 he took the American citizenship. He was married to Sophia Kingdom in 1799, and in 1806 their son Isambard K. Brunel was born – the son will become a famous engineer.

- 6 November – the author is 75.

- 100 years ago, in 1918, the superheterodyne receiver was invented by Edwin Armstrong, 28, (18 December 1890 – 1 February 1954, aged 63.1, American electrical engineer and inventor).

Washington, DC (1790): the entrance to the Smithsonian Institution Building (1849-1855), on Jefferson Drive SW..

<u>2019</u> – Mendeleev, Patrick

- about 2100 years ago, in around 81 BC, the watermill (grain mill) was invented by Greek engineers in Eastern Mediterranean Sea.

- about 1700 years ago, in around 319, the fishing reel was invented in Ancient China, as appears in literary records.

- about 1400 years ago, in around 619, the porcelain was invented during the Tang Dynasty (618 – 907, for 289 years) in China: True porcelain was manufactured in northern China from roughly the beginning of the Tang Dynasty.

- 900 years ago, in 1119, the mariner's compass (wet compass) was invented during the Song Dynasty in China. The typical Chinese navigational compass was in the form of a magnetic needle floating in a bowl of water.

- 6 March – 150 years ago, in 1869, the periodic table of elements was invented by Dmitri Mendeleev, 35, (8 February 1834 – 2 February 1907, aged 72.99, 6 days before 73). He made a formal presentation of his periodic table to the Russian Chemical Society. He formulated the Periodic Law, created a wise version of the periodic table of elements, and used it to correct the properties of some already discovered elements, and also to predict the properties of eight elements yet to be discovered.

- 100 years ago, in 1919, the synthetic route for silica gel was invented and patented by chemistry professor Walter A. Patrick, at Johns Hopkins University, Baltimore, Maryland, USA.

Japan: the east side of Kawaguchiko (6 km^2, 830 m elevation, 100 km south-west of Tokyo, 17 km north of Mt. Fuji), with a bronze statue of a young woman looking at Mount Fuji.

Washington, D.C. (1790): flags on the National Mall, with the Capitol (1793 – 1800, 88 m, center back), and the Smithsonian Institution Building (1849-1855, center right).

Bibliography

"The Histories" by Polybius
"Discours de la Méthode" by René Descartes
"Meditationes de prima philosophia" by René Descartes
"Philosophiae Naturalis Principia Mathematica" by Isaac Newton
Chinese encyclopedia Gujin Tushu Jicheng (Imperial Enciclopaedia)
"Encyclopédie" by Jean-Baptiste le Rond d'Alembert and Denis Diderot
"Encyclopaedia Britannica" by over 4,400 contributors
"Encyclopedia Americana" by Francis Lieber
"Grand Larousse encyclopédique en 24 volumes" by Albert Ducrocq
Nobel Prize Organization
"The Cambridge History of Medicine", edited by Roy Porter
"Great Russian Encyclopedia" by Yury Osipov
"Encyclopedia of China"
"Enciclopedia Italiana di Scienze, Lettere ed Arti" (35 volume), by Giovanni Treccani
"Allgemeine Encyclopädie der Wissenschaften und Künste" by Johann Samuel Ersch und Johann Gottfried Gruber
"Gran Enciclopedia de España"

Michael M. Dediu is also the author of these books (which can be found on Amazon.com):

1. Aphorisms and quotations – with examples and explanations
2. Axioms, aphorisms and quotations – with examples and explanations
3. 100 Great Personalities and their Quotations
4. Professor Petre P. Teodorescu – A Great Mathematician and Engineer
5. Professor Ioan Goia – A Dedicated Engineering Professor

6. Venice (Venezia) – a new perspective. A short presentation with photographs

7. La Serenissima (Venice) - a new photographic perspective. A short presentation with many photos

8. Grand Canal – Venice. A new photographic viewpoint. A short presentation with many photos

9. Piazza San Marco – Venice. A different photographic view. A short presentation with many photos

10. Roma (Rome) - La Città Eterna. A new photographic view. A short presentation with many photos

11. Why is Rome so Fascinating? A short presentation with many photos

12. Rome, Boston and Helsinki. A short photographic presentation

13. Rome and Tokyo – two captivating cities. A short photographic presentation

14. Beautiful Places on Earth – A new photographic presentation

15. From Niagara Falls to Mount Fuji via Rome - A novel photographic presentation

16. From the USA and Canada to Italy and Japan - A fresh photographic presentation

17. Paris – Why So Many Call This City Mon Amour - A lovely photographic presentation

18. The City of Light – Paris (La Ville-Lumière) - A kaleidoscopic photographic presentation

19. Paris (Lutetia Parisiorum) – the romance capital of the world - A kaleidoscopic photographic view

20. Paris and Tokyo – a joyful photographic presentation. With a preamble about the Universe

21. From USA to Japan via Canada – A cheerful photographic documentary

22. 200 Wonderful Places, In The Last 50 Years – A personal photographic documentary

23. Must see places in USA and Japan - A kaleidoscopic photographic documentary

24. Grandeurs of the World - A kaleidoscopic photographic documentary

25. Corneliu Leu – writer on the same wavelength as Mark Twain. An American viewpoint

26. From Berkeley to Pompeii via Rome – A kaleidoscopic photographic documentary

27. From America to Europe via Japan - A kaleidoscopic photographic documentary

28. Discover America and Japan - A photographic documentary

29. J. R. Lucas – philosopher on a creative parallel with Plato, An American viewpoint

30. From America to Switzerland via France - A photographic documentary

31. From Bretton Woods to New York via Cape Cod - A photographic documentary

32. Splendid Places on the Atlantic Coast of the U. S. A. - A photographic documentary

33. Fourteen nice Cities on three Continents - A photographic documentary

34. 17 Picturesque Cities on the World Map - A photographic documentary

35. Unforgettable Places from Four Continents including Trump buildings - A photographic documentary

36. Dediu Newsletter, Volume 1, Number 1, 6 December 2016 – Monthly news, review, comments and suggestions for a better and wiser world

37. Dediu Newsletter, Volume 1, Number 2, 6 January 2017 (available at www.derc.com).

38. Dediu Newsletter, Volume 1, Number 3, 6 February 2017 (available at www.derc.com).

39. London and Greenwich, A photographic documentary

40. Dediu Newsletter, Volume 1, Number 4, 6 March 2017 (available also at www.derc.com).

41. Dediu Newsletter, Volume 1, Number 5, 6 April 2017 (available also at www.derc.com).

42. Dediu Newsletter, Volume 1, Number 6, 6 May 2017 (available also at www.derc.com).

43. Dediu Newsletter, Volume 1, Number 7, 6 June 2017 (available also at www.derc.com).

44. London, Oxford and Cambridge, A photographic documentary

45. Dediu Newsletter, Volume 1, Number 8, 6 July 2017 (available also at www.derc.com).

46. Dediu Newsletter, Volume 1, Number 9, 6 August 2017 (available also at www.derc.com).
47. Dediu Newsletter, Volume 1, Number 10, 6 September 2017 (available also at www.derc.com).
48. Three Great Professors: President Woodrow Wilson, Historian Germán Arciniegas, Mathematician Gheorghe Vrănceanu, A chronological and photographic documentary
49. Dediu Newsletter, Volume 1, Number 11, 6 October 2017 (available also at www.derc.com).
50 Dediu Newsletter, Volume 1, Number 12, 6 November 2017 (available also at www.derc.com).
51 Dediu Newsletter, Volume 2, Number 1 (13), 6 December 2017 (available also at www.derc.com).
52 Two Great Leaders: Augustus and George Washington, A chronological and photographic documentary
53. Dediu Newsletter, Volume 2, Number 2 (14), 6 January 2018 (available also at www.derc.com).
54. Newton, Benjamin Franklin, and Gauss, A chronological and photographic documentary
55. Dediu Newsletter, Volume 2, Number 3 (15), 6 February 2018 (available also at www.derc.com).
56. 2017: World Top Events, But Many Little Known, A chronological and photographic documentary
57. Dediu Newsletter, Volume 2, Number 4 (16), 6 March 2018 (available also at www.derc.com).
58. Vergilius, Horatius, Ovidius, and Shakespeare, A chronological and photographic documentary.
59. Dediu Newsletter, Volume 2, Number 5 (17), 6 April 2018 (available also at www.derc.com).
60. Dediu Newsletter, Volume 2, Number 6 (18), 6 May 2018 (available also at www.derc.com).
61. Vivaldi, Bach, Mozart, and Verdi, A chronological and photographic documentary
62. Dediu Newsletter, Volume 2, Number 7 (19), 6 June 2018 (available also at www.derc.com).
63. Dediu Newsletter, Volume 2, Number 8 (20), 6 July 2018 (available also at www.derc.com).
64. Dediu Newsletter, Volume 2, Number 9 (21), 6 August 2018 (available also at www.derc.com).

65. World History, a new perspective - A chronological and photographic documentary.

66. World Humor History with over 100 Jokes, a new perspective - A chronological and photographic documentary

67. Dediu Newsletter, Vol 2, N 10 (22), 6 September 2018

68. Dediu Newsletter, Vol 2, N 11 (23), 6 October 2018

69. Da Vinci, Michelangelo, Rembrandt, Rodin - A chronological and photographic documentary

70. Dediu Newsletter, Vol 2, N 12 (24), 6 November 2018

71. Dediu Newsletter, Vol 3, N 1 (25), 6 December 2018

72. From Euclid to Edison - revelries in the last 75 years - A chronological and photographic documentary

73. Dediu Newsletter, Vol 3, N 2 (26), 6 January 2019

74. Socrates to Churchill - Aphorisms celebrated after 1960 - A chronological and photographic documentary

75. Dediu Newsletter Vol 3, Number 3 (27), 6 February 2019

76. Hippocrates to Fleming: Medicine History celebrated after 1943 - A chronological and photographic documentary

77. Dediu Newsletter, Volume 3, Number 4 (28), 6 March 2019

78. Dediu Newsletter, Volume 3, Number 5 (29), 6 April 2019

Japan: detail of the north side of Mount Fuji with its peak (3,776 m, 15 km south, 1707 last eruption), from south of Kawaguchiko, 830 m elevation, 100 km south-west of Tokyo.

Michael M. Dediu is the editor of these books (also on Amazon.com):

1. Sophia Dediu: The life and its torrents – Ana. In Europe around 1920
2. Proceedings of the 4th International Conference "Advanced Composite Materials Engineering" COMAT 2012
3. Adolf Shvedchikov: I am an eternal child of spring – poems in English, Italian, French, German, Spanish and Russian
4. Adolf Shvedchikov: Life's Enigma – poems in English, Italian and Russian
5. Adolf Shvedchikov: Everyone wants to be HAPPY – poems in English, Spanish and Russian
6. Adolf Shvedchikov: My Life, My Love – poems in English, Italian and Russian
7. Adolf Shvedchikov: I am the gardener of love – poems in English and Russian
8. Adolf Shvedchikov: Amaretta di Saronno – poems in English and Russian
9. Adolf Shvedchikov: A Russian Rediscovers America
10. Adolf Shvedchikov: Parade of Life - poems in English and Russian
11. Adolf Shvedchikov: Overcoming Sorrow - poems in English and Russian
12. Sophia Dediu: Sophia meets Japan
13. Corneliu Leu: Roosevelt, Churchill, Stalin and Hitler: Their surprising role in Eastern Europe in 1944
14. Proceedings of the 5th International Conference "Computational Mechanics and Virtual Engineering" COMEC 2013
15. Georgeta Simion – Potanga: Beyond Imagination: A Thought-provoking novel inspired from mid-20th century events
16. Ana Dediu: The poetry of my life in Europe and The USA
17. Ana Dediu: The Four Graces
18. Proceedings of the 5th International Conference "Advanced Composite Materials Engineering" COMAT 2014
19. Sophia Dediu: Chocolate Cook Book: Is there such a thing as too much chocolate?

20. Sorin Vlase: Mechanical Identifiability in Automotive Engineering

21. Gabriel Dima: The Evolution of the Aerostructures – Concept and Technologies

22. Proceedings of the 6th International Conference "Computational Mechanics and Virtual Engineering" COMEC 2015

23. Sophia Dediu: Cook Book 1 A-B-C Common sense cooking

24. Sophia Dediu: Dim Sum Spring Festival

25. Ana Dediu and Sophia Dediu: Europe in 1985: A chronological and photographic documentary

26 Stefan Staretu: Europe: Serbian Despotate of Srem and the Romanian area. Between the 14th and the 16th Centuries

Japan: the north side of Mount Fuji (3,776 m, 17 km south, 1707 last eruption) seen from the north-east side of Lake Kawaguchi, 6 km^2, 830 m elevation, 100 km south-west of Tokyo.

USA, Newport, the Ochre Court (1892, 50 rooms, Ogden Goelet (1851-1897, real estate), donated in 1947 to Salve Regina College (1934), in 1991 University status, with this administrative building.

USA, Newport, Vinland Estate (1882, C. L. Wolfe (1828-1887), with a large Roman dolium (200 BC) near the main entrance, donated in 1955 to Salve Regina University (1934) and renamed McAuley Hall.

www.ingramcontent.com/pod-product-compliance
Lightning Source LLC
Chambersburg PA
CBHW041310210326
41599CB00003B/48